Semiotic Animal

A postmodern definition of human being

transcending Patriarchy and Feminism

Other titles of interest from St. Augustine's Press

Semiotic Animal

A postmodern definition of human being
transcending Patriarchy and Feminism

to supersede the ancient and medieval 'animal rationale'
along with the modern 'res cogitans'

John Deely

South Bend, IN: St. Augustine's Press 2010

Library of Congress Cataloging-in-Publication Data
Deely, John N.
Semiotic animal: a postmodern definition of "human being"
transcending Patriarchy and Feminism/ John Deely.
p. cm.
Includes bibliographical references (p.   ) and index.
ISBN-13: 978-1-58731-758-3 (alk. paper)
ISBN-10: 1-58731-758-3 (alk. paper)
1. Semiotics—Philosophy. I. Title.
P99.4.S62D45 2010
302.201—dc22   2009036701

Photo on main title page:
Author in the old church Santa María de la Asunción, winter of 1966,
in the neighborhood of Santa María Ahuacatitlán,
outlying Cuernavaca, Mexico, accompanied by
Osso and his brother Béthoven, two of the neighborhood dogs

A preliminary shorter version of this work was published privately
for the 2005 Semiotics Seminar series
conducted at the Southeast European Center for Semiotic Studies
of the New Bulgarian University in Sofia, Bulgaria
where the author was a Visiting Fulbright Professor of semiotics and philosophy

This work is dedicated
to the two before me
and one after me
who introduced this expression "semiotic animal" as an original coinage,
if only in passing.
In the present essay is brought down to earth and systematized,
now, this expression that has been "in the air"
since Peirce's semiotic reformulation
of the ancient discussion of categories.
That this new understanding of human being
transcends alike Patriarchy and Feminism
was the original insight of Brooke Williams Deely,
as Chapter 12 attests.

Contents:

The Gestation of This Work

Between 1990 (where the expression "semiotic animal" occurs in the opening second paragraph and the concluding final paragraph of my book the *Basics of Semiotics*) and my preparation of an earlier version of this work (for private publication in the 2005 Semiotics Seminar Series of the Southeast European Center for Semiotic Studies) I have returned to this subject no less than seven times, but only in essay form. Each of the nine total mentions[1] has been a little different, according to the occasion, developing new points and differently emphasizing earlier ones. But here I want to bring everything together as a whole in monographic form, to indicate how fully to comprehend this notion of "semiotic animal" as more than a passing expression popping up here and there, with an intent to establish the expression *as a usage* expressly in the framework of the development of semiotics, the doctrine of signs, as the positive "postmodern turn" in philosophy's long history.

My own first usage of the expression in question was a coinage, made in passing, as it were; and I have since learned (as will also the reader of these pages) that, also independently, at least two before me[2]

---

[1] See Deely 1990, 2003a 2003b, 2003c, 2004a, 2004b, 2005c, 2005d, 2005e.

[2] Mongré (aka Hausdorff) 1897: 7: "Der Mensch ist ein semiotisches Tier" — "The human being is a semiotic animal"; Rossi-Landi 1978: 217 (p. 347 in the 2005 Ponzio edition): "L'uomo, quale animale semiotico, è semiotico per intero" — "The human being, as a semiotic animal, is semiotic through and through".

and one after me[3] coined the same expression without making a full theoretical development to establish the usage. No doubt, with the 21st century development of semiotics according to the full scope of semiosis as the action of signs (appearing as it now does to be coextensive with the universe itself in the realm of physical interactions[4]), we will find that this notion of "semiotic animal" will be, more and more, "in the air"; so it seems to me high time expressly to thematize the notion and to establish conceptually its most proper usage. That is the aim of this little book.

The development of semiotic consciousness in so fundamental an aspect is too important to entrust only to the passing breeze, for the understanding of the human being as the only semiotic animal on earth is central to semiotic advance. A work even as small as this one, if it establishes that central point, will go far to assist semiotics to sink ever deeper roots into the intellectual culture as postmodern, despite skeptics, nay-sayers, and territorial concerns of traditional academics seeking to preserve their "boundaries" (and hence unable to be comfortable with the study of a form of being — the sign strictly considered — which leads everywhere in nature and culture alike, crossing all boundaries, yes, but only while giving the means to show in what ways the boundaries are legitimate in the first place).

The argument of this work, then, seeks to show how semiotics provides the dawn of a new understanding of the human being as no mere 'thinking thing' but a veritable part of the whole of nature, a *semiotic animal*, charged as such, for reasons that come more and more to the fore, even with the *care* of nature, the responsibility for the health of life on the planet as a whole ("semioethics"), as it is turning out.

---

[3] Petrilli 1998: 3, 181–182. It was in 2002, as a conference in Milan, that Petrilli, Ponzio, and Deely began to work together to establish "semiotic animal" not just as a passing expression, but as established usage for semiotic development (see Deely, Petrilli, and Ponzio 2005).

[4] Deely 2008 (now also Reading 3 in Cobley ed. 2009: 74–90), 2008a; and see the "Timeline of Semiotic Development" in Deely 2009: Appendix E, 237–246.

One point for the reader to bear in mind from the outset concerns the style in which the argument is presented: frequent but relatively informal and unexplained use with unusual connotations of such terms as "thing" and "object", "cathectic" vs. "cognitive", "cenoscopic" vs. "ideoscopic",[5] early on in the work are unavoidable, yet the reader who persists to the end will find the unsettling connotations fully clarified and justified by the end of the book.

Here too, perhaps, is the place to mention a neologism introduced into my analysis from the Latin semiotic of John Poinsot, namely, the English verb-form *provenate*. This verb in English derives from the Latin infinitive 'provenire', to come or issue forth, appear, arise, be produced; its closest relative in existing English being the noun-form "provenance" ("where something originated or was nurtured in its early existence"). Hence, as will appear, a relation *provenates* from its fundament only *contingently* in *ens reale* restrictively conceived, but *necessarily* when the fundament is a psychological state. Thus, as psychological states cannot be without being 'of' or 'about' something other than themselves, so as qualities they belong to subjectivity as entangled inescapably with suprasubjectivity, but they do not depend upon a *subjectively existing terminus* in order to give rise to relations. In this case, the relation *provenates* — i.e., issues forth from or 'on the foundation of' the psychological quality — *necessarily* regardless of any subjectivity on the side of its terminus; for just as terminus as terminus and fundament as fundament equally depend upon the suprasubjective being of relation *alike* when the terminus *also* has a subjective dimension *and* when it does *not* have such a dimension, when a quality — besides being subjectively inherent — is a fundament necessarily and so not just contingently gives rise to an actual relation, that relation *in turn*, while making the fundament a fundament (as formally distinct even though materially

---

[5] The spelling variants of these terms (notably "cœnoscopic" and "idioscopic") as perhaps more correct etymologically I have discussed in the opening paragraph of Chapter 1 in Deely 2008b: 3, and will not repeat the discussion here.

identical with the subjective state as inherent accident founding the relation), cannot be except as *also* making a terminus, even though that terminus is only contingently and not necessarily *further* given subjectively as an instantiation in its own right of the subjective dimension of *ens reale*. Relations which arise contingently, the only kind considered in Aristotle's circumscription of relation as an irreducible categorial mode of το ὸν, in other words, *necessarily* have a terminus which is *also* a subjective accident; but the necessity in the case directly bears only on the question of the relation's *intersubjectivity*, not its presupposed and more basic *suprasubjectivity*, without which latter "feature" it could not be a relation at all, but with which it may, or may not, depending solely upon circumstances, be intersubjective *as well*. As we will see, especially in Chapter 8 (notably Section 8.3.), this is the "*singularity*" of relation which makes semiosis, or the action of signs, possible in the first place, because it is the ground of the prior possibility of the being of signs which semiosis is consequent upon, and which also provides (in anthroposemiosis) the ground of the prior possibility of that conformity between "thought" and "thing" in which truth consists. But here is the occasion only to make the terminological point of how I have introduced "provenate" as an English verb, leaving the theoretical implications and context of the stipulation for the body of the work to follow.

It is an old problem: by using familiar terms in an unfamiliar way, one upsets the hearer; by inventing entirely new terms one risks to lose the hearer completely. Yet there is no alternative to getting new ideas across: one must either use old words in new ways, or invent new words and try to get enough of the old ways of thinking "on board" to see matters in a new light, or achieve some effective combination of the two. I go this third way, mindful of the admonition I heard in my teenage years from Bishop Fulton Sheen: "You can't simultaneously educate people and cater to their ignorance".

For the semiotic animal is just that: a whole new way of seeing human being, that must yet be shown to cast more traditional understandings in this new light if it is to "catch on". I have tried to strike a balance between introducing new terms and using familiar terms in unfamiliar ways, precisely to craft the new understanding. The reader needs but two things in order reach the new understanding — *patience* with puzzling uses on first appearance, and *persistence* to the end, by which combination he or she will more likely than not see by the end just how the pieces of the puzzle fit together in a new picture of human "being in the world", a picture amply illustrating Ratzinger's claim (1970: 132) that "the undivided sway of thinking in terms of substance is ended; relation is discovered as an equally valid primordial mode of reality" — and this throughout the whole of nature, wherever semiosis is at work, even if especially in bringing to full florescence (through metasemiosis) the being proper to human animals as semiotic.

Interestingly, this same author, Joseph Ratzinger, now writing as Pope Benedict XVI, having earlier addressed the main subject presupposed to semiosis, namely, relation as a primordial reality of nature co-terminus with individuality, now (2009: Chap. 4, esp. ¶s 36, 45, 48, 50–51) has addressed also the subject of our "Sequel" in the present volume, namely, semioethics. He notes that "the adjective 'ethical'" requires recognition that the responsibility proper to ethics is (¶50) "a global one", based on (¶48) "a 'grammar'" *within the environment* which places nature as including ourselves rightly "at our disposal" only on the basis of an action of signs.[6] Only through the mastery of this "grammar" can human animals draw the principles which separate wise use from reckless exploitation, in the realization that the consequences of behavior include but extend well beyond social and cultural interactions as such — the traditional "ethics" of individual human behavior and species-specifically human social interaction. This treatment called for by Benedict, thus, lacks only the name for "an ethics stringently derived from semiosis" (in the felicitous expression formulated off-

---

   [6] Benedict XVI (Ratzinger) 2009: ¶48: "Natura ... signavit intrinsecas ordinationes ut homo ex iis percipiat debitas normas".

hand by Jeff Bernard at the 10th World Congress of the International Association for Semiotic Studies, held in Spain less than three months after the publication of Benedict's encyclical letter).

John Deely

final manuscript submitted 23 September 2009
A Coruña, Galicia, Spain

Semiotic Animal

A postmodern definition of human being

transcending Patriarchy and Feminism

Chapter 1

A Question from On High

Sometime in the year 1999, as I recall, I received from my good friend Ralph McInerny at Notre Dame University in South Bend a telephone call in which he urged me to read the papal encyclical *Fides et Ratio*. "Just go to Yahoo and type in 'Vatican'," he instructed me, "and follow the indications." I did, downloaded and read the encyclical, and discovered to my astonishment that the book I was then completing, in effect, addressed directly the then-Pope's concern as to how, from within philosophy, the term "postmodern" ought to be understood. For it was Wojtyła's contention that the philosophical sense that must be given to the term "postmodern" depends on an adequate answer being given at the same time to "the delicate question of the demarcation of the different historical periods".

The reason for this contention is not far to seek. For inevitably, as Professor Kenneth Schmitz has pointed out,[1] "the term 'post-modernity' is parasitic upon the meaning given to the term 'modernity'." Exactly "when is modernity supposed to have ended?", Schmitz asked pointedly; "And in what is modernity supposed to have consisted?" Whoever cannot answer these questions is in no position to speak more than nominalistically of anything

---

[1] Schmitz 1990: 153–154.

"postmodern" in philosophy. Perhaps coincidentally, Professor Schmitz had the privilege of an unusually close intellectual interaction with the Pope himself over the course of some annual seminars in the years closing the 20th century and opening the 21st.

Meanwhile my book demarcating the four ages of philosophical culture down to the present time had been finally published in 2001. So, when I had the chance to be in Rome from September 20–26 of 2003 as participant (speaking on the topic of human beings as semiotic animals) in the International Congress "Christian Humanism in the Third Millennium" that had been convened at the behest of John-Paul II himself, I used my ecclesiastical connections, such as they are, to ensure that I would be able to attend an audience with the Holy Father for the purpose of presenting to him in person an inscribed copy of my book addressing his question of the demarcation of the philosophical epochs sufficient to determine the proper sense in which "postmodernity" is to have a more than nominalistic meaning within intellectual culture insofar as philosophy is involved.

My connections in Rome proved good enough to ensure me a place in any one of three different papal audiences in the Vatican schedule, and I looked forward to presenting Pope John-Paul II with the inscribed copy of my book opened to the very page 589 whereon his encyclical of 1998 is cited on the matter of "how the designation 'postmodern' ought to be received and established within 'the philosophical field'." Imagine my dismay as, one after another, the three audiences were cancelled in turn by papal illness. Talk about bad luck.

I had to entrust the task of ensuring delivery of my book to a new friend in the Dominican order, Friar Edward Kaczynski, O.P., then-Rector (though I was unaware of the fact) of the Pontifical University of St. Thomas Aquinas in Rome (the Angelicum). A letter acknowledging the gift to Pope John-Paul II arrived in Houston many weeks later, so I know my friend was reliable; but I suppose that now I will never know whether Karol Wojtyła in person actually saw the use I had made of his question, or what, if anything, he made of my answer to the question as he had posed it. C'est la vie.

Chapter 2

The Answer Given in Advance:
the Owl of Wisdom Flies toward Evening

My proposal is that modern philosophy began when Descartes made a construct of the mind the direct object of experience, a starting point reaffirmed by Locke with his "ideas of sensation", and embraced by Kant in his doctrine of the sensory manifold. My reason is that this doctrine that the human mind from the first actively constructs objectivity directly experienced proved to be the quintessence of idealism as modern philosophy came to understand 'epistemology' or the 'theory of knowledge'. The "linguistic turn" in 20th century analytic philosophy only tightened this embrace of the proposition in question, and the phenomenological turn in the same period to "the things themselves" did not succeed in ending that embrace, though it certainly took the late modern heirs of rationalism a long ways in the right direction.[1]

Yet it remains that, from Descartes to Wittgenstein and Husserl, modernity has considered that the being of the things in themselves as they are in themselves independently of relations to ourselves is, more likely than not, "unknowable". The Kantian demarcation of the boundaries of the knowable is classic modern: on the side of sensation, the unknowable is the *Ding an sich*, the thing-in-itself; and

---

[1] The work of Sokolowski (e.g., 2002) is exemplary of the possibilities.

on the side of conception, the unknowable is the *Noumenon*, the concept with an object irreducible to sensory intuition — whence the modern claim that God, the soul, and the world of nature are "unknowable" by the human mind, which can only think as it must about its own constructs from beginning to end.

The term "realism" in philosophy has many meanings, some of which border on idiotic, but the central one was in another pope's mind when, in 1879, then-Pope Leo XIII issued an *imperium* to the higher education mission of the Catholic Church to restore the philosophy of St. Thomas Aquinas according to which precisely the Kantian limits both on the side of sense and on the side of intellection are not accepted, so that precisely a knowledge of the subjective constitution of the things as they are in themselves and of the reality of God and the human soul are not only possible but the natural goal and terminus of the full development of human understanding. So, over the later 19th century and most of the 20th century, came to be defined the struggle between, in the modern sense, "realism" and "idealism", as witnessed in the works of thinkers as diverse as Jacques Maritain and Paul Ricoeur, Bernard Lonergan and Maurice Merleau-Ponty.

When exactly did it end, this contest between the modern realists and modern idealists? It ended, in principle, twelve years prior to Pope Leo XIII's call, in 1867,[2] when Charles Sanders Peirce proposed his "New List of Categories" in which — no longer, as

---

[2] The situation reminds me of a seminar on papal social teachings conducted in the 1963–1964 academic year at the Dominican House of Studies in River Forest, Illinois, by my mentor in philosophy, Ralph Austin Powell (1914–2001). A session of the seminar was visited unexpectedly by one of the 'periti' of the Second Vatican Council. Three students presented papers at that session, but all had the theme that papal social teachings tended to fall into the category of "too little, too late" throughout the modern period. Fr Powell grew increasingly uncomfortable with the student tone in the presence of this distinguished emissary of the Dominican Master General (not to say the Vatican), and in his final summary tried to put the best face on the student critiques of the papal social teachings. "That such teachings would often be belated", he said, "should be understood in the light of Hegel's saying that 'The Owl of Wisdom always flies towards evening'." Whatever the Roman representative thought of the whole matter I never learned.

in Aristotle, was the aim to classify all and only the possible modes of mind-independent being; and no longer, as in Kant, was the aim to demonstrate that only modes of mind-dependent being can be directly experienced and to determine what those modes are (the "a-prioris") — the aim was to classify the manner in which mind-dependent being and mind-independent being interpenetrate and reveal themselves objectively through the weave and pattern of human experience as consisting of and constituted by the relations in which signs consist and through which the activity of signs, or "semiosis", extends in principle to *the whole of being* as "knowable".[3]

It was a going forward and not a going back, and hence neither a "realism" in the modern sense calling for the restoration against modernity of an earlier philosophical view, nor an "idealism" in the modern sense of asserting that everything known or knowable is a construct of human understanding. The categories of semiosis were a definitively *postmodern* setting of the terms of the intellectual discussion of objectivity on the basis of the understanding of sign as transcending in its proper being and activity the ancient divide between φυσις and νομος and no less the modern divide between self ("inner") and world ("outer") — between a misconceived objectivity and a solipsistic subjectivity. And the name for this new point of view Peirce took (so it would seem) from Locke: the *doctrina signorum* or *semiotica* — semiotics, according to which the medieval maxim that *ens et verum convertuntur* is restored in the formula that the action of signs establishes a "coincidence of communication with being".[4]

To the modern question of the debate between idealism and realism as — like the being pregnant of any given woman admitting of no third possibility — requiring a "yes" or "no", the doctrine of signs advanced an unequivocal "yes", that "there is no doubt that the inner human world, with great effort and serious study, may reach an understanding of non-human worlds and of its

---

[3] See the fuller discussion and enumeration of Peirce's "final list" of the new categories in Chapter 4 below, Section 4.2., from p. 17 to end.

[4] Petrilli and Ponzio 2001: 54.

connection with them".[5] As Peirce put it, "scholastic realism" is of the essence of semiotics, incompatible with nominalism in every form,[6] *but not sufficient for semiotics.*

For the doctrine of signs not only restores the knowability of the subjective constitution of *ens reale* put 'under erasure' in the mainstream modern versions of "epistemology" (which was the sole aim and over-riding preoccupation of the modern "realist" debate with "idealism"); the doctrine of signs also recognizes full well and accounts directly for the huge measure of reality as *socially constructed* by the traditions of animal life in general and including in particular the traditions of human animal life known as "culture", which is but the species-specifically human development of nature consequent upon linguistic communication. Thus, without being at all *indifferent* to the modern "realism vs. idealism" debate, semiotics starts at a point which is precisely *beyond* that debate in the terms which modernity set for it.

In philosophy, semiotics acknowledges no pre-existing paradigm, but forges for knowledge and experience its own paradigm, the paradigm worked out directly from study of the being of signs as revealed by the cenoscopic study of the actions which reveal that being in its singularity.

Students of semiotics need to read the works of the philosophers in this light, and to bear well in mind that the mainstream modern philosophers down to and through the 20th century twilight of modernity who, almost[7] to a man and woman, *knew nothing and read nothing* of the main period of protosemiotic development as it took place between William of Ockham (c.1285–1349) and

---

[5] Petrilli and Ponzio 2001: 20.

[6] Which was exactly why Peirce urged the adoption of the term "pragmaticism" in place of his earlier coinage "pragmatism" to separate his followers from the nominalism which was a part of the essence of philosophy in the modern period. See Deely 2001: Chap. 15; and the Red and Green Books at <http://www.helsinki.fi/science/commens/papers.html>.

[7] The only exception truly notable was Jacques Maritain, e.g., in his writings on signs between 1937 and 1957, but with many critical passages throughout his other writings as well. See Deely 1986; Sebeok 1989a, 1989b.

John Poinsot (1589–1644). Instead, philosophers of the modern period have made their own the Cartesian fiction that authors of the late Latin period had nothing of interest to say.

Modern ignorance on this point of the original florescence of semiotic consciousness in the protosemiotic development from Augustine to Poinsot can be demonstrated by consulting any of the histories of philosophy that became standard in the 20th century. All of them subscribe more or less explicitly to the opinion Matson states as late as 1987:[8] "William of Ockham was the last of the great creative scholastics. The three centuries following his death are a philosophical desert." Yet precisely these are the three centuries in which the maturity of the first florescence of semiotic consciousness, the "protosemiotic development", was reached, planting the seed which was not to blossom in its proper potential for another three centuries — the period of modern philosophy, which was, from a semiotic point of view, a "cryptosemiotic interlude", as not allowing in the general intellectual culture for a scope of human knowledge such as the action of signs makes possible in fact.

And the situation is actually worse than this. For the very professors who populate the philosophy departments as the 21st century opens, the first fully postmodern century from a semiotic point of view, are aware almost as little of the late 20th century blossoming of the second semiotic consciousness (after Peirce's re-covery of the late Latins) as their predecessors were of the proto-semiotic authors.

Hence the modern philosophers as a collectivity should be regarded by the students of semiotics, and for some considerable time to come, with at least as much healthy skepticism as Descartes urged upon the early moderns in their reading of the Latin think-ers before the time of Galileo: they may deserve to be read, "but at the same time there is a considerable danger that if we study these

---

[8] Matson 1987: II, 253. Desmond FitzGerald (1986a: 430) has rightly char-acterized this remark as "an absurd comment". Yet its absurdity does not gainsay its accuracy as a summation of the standardized attitude toward and treatment of Latin thought of the late fourteenth to early seventeenth century.

works too closely traces of their errors will infect us and cling to us against our will and despite our precautions."[9] Just as in politics you cannot effect a revolution and at the same time preserve the *ancien régime*, so in intellectual culture you cannot develop what is new simply by repeating or extending the old.

The revolution the protosemiotic development called for in philosophy went astray in the actual direction that the modern revolution took.[10] That is not unusual — for a revolution to take a wrong turn. But the time of the sign has finally come, and the work of the protosemioticians is not to be in vain after all.

Semiotics could have been the direction of the modern revolution in philosophy to accompany what has turned out to be the true modern revolution (namely, the ideoscopic development of science in the modern sense — Dr. Jekyll to modern philosophy's Mr. Hyde, as I have put it[11]), but it was not. The semiotic revolution had to wait instead for modernity in philosophy to run its course, and for the artificial limits modern epistemology imposed on the human spirit to become intolerable, to become veritably an *ancien régime*.

The postmodern revolution in philosophy — the semiotic revolution — is the reclaiming within the doctrine of signs the heritage and challenge of the protosemiotic development, a development which, as I have shown at some length,[12] was no less of a challenge to traditional natural philosophy and metaphysics in Galileo's time than it has proved to be to modern epistemology and critical philosophy in our own time.

---

[9] Descartes 1628: 13.

[10] See Deely 1994: Part I; Deely 2001: Part II; and 2009: Sections 11 & 12 — the protosemiotic challenge backward and forward.

[11] Deely 2001: Chap. 13.

[12] Deely 2009: Sections 11–15.

Chapter 3

The New Understanding
of Human Being

I would guess there was something "in the air". When modern philosophy broke with traditional metaphysics and natural philosophy, it did so, as we have seen, in full ignorance of the protosemiotic development that had accompanied, but not been central, to the development of natural philosophy in the Aristotelian sense of physics from the time of Albert the Great to the Galilean revolution. The "turn to the subject" resulting in the conception of human being as a *res cogitans* provided a formula which caught early the essence of the modern revolution, if not in science, at least in philosophy.

So it is not surprising that within thirty years of Peirce's break with modern philosophy we find the first occurrence of the formula that will catch the essence of the postmodern revolution: "Der Mensch ist ein semiotisches Thier" — the human being is a semiotic animal.[1] What is strange in this case is that it would be another full ninety-three years before this formula would surface again, and only after that be seized upon to express the essence of the postmodern human identity.

It is to that matter that we turn in the pages to follow.

---

[1] Hausdorff/Mongré 1897: 7.

Chapter 4

Vienna Prologue:[1] A Glance at the Development as a Whole within which the Semiotic Animal Debuts[2]

The 20th century proved to be the decisive one for the establishment, after all these long centuries of human habitation of the earth, of a thematic and systematic awareness of the dependence of knowledge through experience upon the action of signs. Over the decades of the 20th century, slow by slow, the idealistic heritage was transcended in the establishment of semiotics as a doctrine of signs which neither merely recycled the realism vs. idealism debates of the late modern era, nor proposed a throwback to the scholastic realism of high medieval times.

---

[1] I was invited, and accepted with great delight, to address the question of the "semiotic animal" at the 18 March 2005 Wiener Semiotische Konversationen and Birthday Celebration in honor of Gloria Withalm, IASS Honorary President, General Secretary of the Institute for Socio-Semiotic Studies, Vienna, and the Austrian Semiotic Society. This section of the present booklet, thus, comes directly from that occasion, and I have used this Vienna text also to form Part I of Deely 2005b.

[2] The first version of this paper to distinguish between *symbolic animal* as generic and *semiotic animal* as specific appeared in the *American Catholic Philosophical Quarterly* 79.3 (Deely 2005d). The earliest occurrence of the expression "semiotic animal" in English seems to have been Deely 1990: 2, 24n7, and 124. The earliest use of this expression to develop a definitional formula occurs in Deely 1995, followed, but completely independently, by Petrilli 1998: 8, 181–182; and, again independently, in Deely 2001: 680, 736–737, and Deely 2002: 124–125, 2002a. After 2003 the English and the Italian usages of the expression as definitional become interactive. See Petrilli 2003; Deely 2004a and 2004b; and Deely, Petrilli, and Ponzio 2005.

Instead, semiotics, by focusing on the being proper to signs, proved to have introduced a whole new standpoint and paradigm or model for debate, through which participants in the development gradually came to realize that the question of the being proper to sign transcends the very terms in which the modern philosophical debate was to develop. For the being and action of signs constitutes not a distinct realm but an interface between the distinct realms of nature and culture, an interface thanks to which, depending on circumstances (always varying), the inquirer into signs cannot avoid being led now into the realms of nature, now into the realms of culture, now into the interlacing of both in the objects of experience themselves formed by and dependent upon that general action of signs we now recognize as "semiosis" and in which the human being participates but does not by any means constitute *omni ex parte* through its "anthroposemiosis".

4.1. Semiology

The development was neither linear nor smooth — revolutions seldom are. The greatest obstacle proved to be the initial adoption by the majority of inquirers into signs of a definition and a model for the signifying process which was "arbitrary" in the invidious sense of resting upon a *stipulation*, upon the adoption of a convention which stifled, by artificially limiting, the very inquiry it purported to support. For instead of approaching the being of signs through the consideration of their action as observable and analyzable in the experience of all of us, Saussure rather stipulated that the sign — not *some signs*, but the *sign itself, the sign as such* — is linguistic in essence and dyadic in character, being constituted by the external relation of acoustic image, or signifier (*signifiant*), to concept, or signified (*signifié*), a relation which is transparently not motivated by anything that analysis can reveal in the constitution itself of either of the two elements related: neither in the constitution of the *signifiant*, nor in the constitution of the *signifié*.[3]

---

[3] For the full context of Saussure's dyadic model in the overall development of semiotics over the decades of the 20th century, see Deely 2009d and 2009e.

Perhaps it was the consonance of such a proposal with the idealist mindset of modernity, introduced by Descartes's notion of essential humanity as a *res cogitans* to which the natural world is compared as "external", an externality ruthlessly systemized under the rubric of "unknowable" in the critical philosophy of Immanuel Kant which dominated modernity to the very end (which means to this very day in departments of philosophy institutionally blind to the postmodern development of the doctrine of signs). Whatever the reason, however, the arbitrary model of sign stipulated by Saussure as the keystone in the arch of any study of signs was embraced on all hands, and the name Saussure proposed for the new study, semiology, was embraced in Western Europe and America along with the arbitrary model.

Now Saussure was certainly right in his pointing out that the thematic study of signs did not exist in modern culture, but had (as he put it) "a right to existence and a place staked out in advance".[4]

But Saussure's own proposal for launching sign studies so radically misconceived and distorted that "place marked out in advance" that it took about nine of the 20th century's ten decades to begin to commence to start to straighten things out. In the process, what gradually came clear to the inquirers was that they were witnesses to nothing less than the death of modernity as an epoch in philosophy, and the gestation of an epoch as new vis-à-vis modernity as modernity had been new vis-à-vis the Latin scholasticism of the medieval epoch. Yet semiology, on its own terms, lacked the capacity to cross the new frontier of which the growing awareness of signs was drawing the contours ever more clearly. The semiologists found themselves, like Moses, stranded in the desert, deprived of the means of entry fully into the Promised Land, tangled in the artificial constraints of their own nominal definitions.

---

[4] Saussure 1916: 16: "Puisqu'elle n'existe pas encore, on ne peut dire ce qu'elle sera; mais elle a droit à l'existence. Sa place est déterminée d'avance." — "Since a science of signs does not yet exist, one cannot say exactly what form it will take; but it has a right to existence. Its place is staked out in advance."

4.2. The Time of the Sign

Yet the study of signs was something whose time had come, even if its integral development as an intellectual project proved to require nothing less than a blasting away of the very foundations upon which modernity had erected its idea of "critical philosophy" and "epistemology", in contrast with the discredited "ontology" of medieval (not to mention ancient) times. The very idea of an "external world" as modernity had proposed it soon enough manifested itself, to the eyes of inquirers into the action of signs, as a quasi-fallacy,[5] a blunder *ab initio*.

For while there assuredly is a physical universe which is 'external to' in the sense of surrounding us as bodily creatures limited in "extension" (i.e., in the occupation of *ubi circumscriptivum* — the exact bodily location of a material substance in the surrounding world of bodies, Aristotle's sense of "where" in his list of the ways in which beings can exist mind-independently), not only are we as biological organisms part of this universe, but also is this physical universe properly regarded as "external" only insofar as and to the extent that it forms no part of our awareness at any given time. For whatever we are aware of, insofar as we are aware of it, is internal to our consciousness, not external to it in the manner postulated by the moderns (and deemed unknowable by Kant). Heidegger evinced this with his notion of *Dasein*,[6] thus pointing the way from

---

[5] Sebok 1984: 76; Deely 2003: Part II.

[6] Heidegger 1927: 89: "When Dasein directs itself towards something and grasps it, it does not somehow first get out of an inner sphere in which it has been proximally encapsulated, but its primary kind of Being is such that it is always 'outside' alongside entities which it encounters and which belong to a world already discovered. Nor is any inner sphere abandoned when Dasein dwells alongside the entity to be known, and determines its character; but even in this 'Being-outside' alongside the object, Dasein is still 'inside', if we understand this in the correct sense; that is to say, it is itself 'inside' as a Being-in-the-world which knows. And furthermore, the perceiving of what is known is not a process of returning with one's booty to the 'cabinet' of consciousness after one has gone out and grasped it; even in perceiving, retaining, and preserving, the Dasein which knows *remains outside*, and it does so *as Dasein*. ... Even the forgetting of something ... must be conceived *as a modification of the primordial Being-in*; and this holds for every delusion and for every error."

within philosophy itself toward the inevitability of an epoch of intellectual culture beyond the modern;[7] but the resulting *Seinsphilosophie* yet shared the semiological limitation of being cast in terms fundamentally applicable only to the situation of the human animal in its species-specific uniqueness.

Already in 1867 Charles Peirce had proposed a new system of categories which, in contrast with Aristotle's system, did not purport to enumerate or classify only the ways in which being can exist independently of the human mind; and, in contrast with Kant's system, did not purport to demonstrate that the ways in which being can be thought are thoroughly determined by the a-priori structures of the pure reason imposing necessary order on the chaos of sensory stimulations. Instead, Peirce proposed a system of categories purporting to show how, within human awareness, both mind-dependent and mind-independent objective being comes to exist and be known through the action of signs.

The "New List" did not fall from heaven full-blown. In fact, work upon it can be traced as early as 1857, when Peirce was barely eighteen years of age. And in his formal proposal of 1867, age twenty-seven, he enumerated the categories as five in number, and not till the 1880s did he set out the final enumeration of the categories as only but irreducibly threefold (and named accordingly as Firstness, Secondness, and Thirdness). I call Peirce's final enumeration *semiotic categories*, or the *categories of experience*, because precisely what they do is account for the transformation of the animal Umwelt into the human Lebenswelt. The simplicity of the scheme exhibits the same kind of genius we find in the history of semiotic at the point when Poinsot realized that, by framing the question of sign in terms of the contrast between transcendental and ontological relative, he had hit upon an exclusive and exhaustive alternative wherein the choice became a self-evident one, precisely because the sign transcends the traditional division of being into mind-independent *ens reale* and mind-dependent *ens rationis*, while only

---

[7] In Deely 2001, see pp. 344ff.

the ontological relative, *relation secundum esse*, as Thomas termed it, admits of positive verification in both orders.[8]

The reason why Peirce finally assigns his categories the names of Firstness, Secondness, and Thirdness, becomes apparent as the manner in which the categories function unfolds. Experience moves the understanding from a confused total grasp wherein there is no difference between dream and reality, possibility and actuality — because all is wrapped up in one "blooming, buzzing confusion" (*Firstness*, what Thomas calls "ens primum cognitum" in his analogy comparing the possible intellect in the order of knowledge to prime matter in the order of material being) — to definite experiences and conceptions wherein the determinate plurality of the physical environs intrudes (*Secondness* — *brute* Secondness) into the objective whole, but then sooner or later becomes *intelligible* through sign relations (*Thirdness*).

Thus Firstness is the *primum cognitum* of Aquinas left over as a free-floating problem from the 13th century,[9] but one now situated determinately at the base of the doctrine of signs, while Secondness is the realm of action and passion in Aristotle's list of the

---

[8] As Poinsot summarized in his *Tractatus de Signis* of 1632: 53/37–45, "Sola vero relatio, quia non dicit solum conceptum 'in', sed etiam conceptum 'ad', ratione cuius praecise non dicit existentiam in se, sed extrinsecam termini attingentiam, ideo non repugnat concipi sine realitate, atque adeo ut ens rationis, concipiendo illud non ut in alio vel ut in se, sed ut ad aliud cum negatione existentiae in aliquo." — "The singularity of relation arises from the fact that relation alone, because it bespeaks not only the notion of 'being in' something, but also the notion of 'being toward' another (by reason precisely of which notion relation bespeaks not an existence in itself but an existence which attains extrinsically a terminus), for this reason a relation conceived remains a relation even without any mind-independent status, and therefore when it exists as a mind-dependent being, because to recognize that a relation is mind-dependent involves conceiving the relation in question neither as having being in another nor being in itself, but only as having a being toward with the concomitant judgmental recognition that the subjective requirements for a relation to have a mind-independent being toward are not here and now fulfilled."

[9] See my essays on "Unmasking Objectivity", 2009g and 2010. Also *Purely Objective Reality* (Deely 2009a) and "The Problem of Being as First Known" in Deely 2001: 341–357.

categories of το όν as *ens reale* but precisely as such interaction involves the sensory awareness of human animals, and Thirdness is the realm where "ens et verum convertuntur" by the intellect's adding to animal *phantasiari* the relation of self-identity needed to sever the exclusive relevance of objects perceived to the perceiving organism, as I have set out at length in treating of *Intentionality and Semiotics*.[10]

The date regarded in Peirce scholarship as the first, so to say, "official" proposal of these semiotic categories, then — May 14, 1867 — can justly be assigned as the beginning of postmodernity.[11] For how else, for the present, are we to name the philosophical epoch in which a way was opened beyond the modern idea that all knowable reality was somehow a humanly constructed reality beyond which (behind the veil of the phenomena) the 'things-in-themselves' remained forever unknown and unknowable in their own constitution?

4.3. The 'Way of Signs'

As far as we know, despite their contemporaneity in life, Saussure and Peirce seem to have had no acquaintance with one another. Both got onto the way of signs quite independently, but only Peirce did so in a way that got him definitively off the Way of Ideas. Where Saussure and the semiologists determinedly lingered over the middle decades of the 20th century along this by-then-old-and-familiar way, decades which were dominated by their discourse, others engaged in the study of signs gradually came together in the realization that the Way of Signs is neither old nor familiar in the themes of intellectual culture, philosophy, and human consciousness, but something decidedly new in its possibilities and demands for thought.

---

[10] Deely 2007.

[11] See Part IV of the *Four Ages of Understanding*, "Postmodern Times. The Way of Signs" (Deely 2001), pp. 609–742, but especially Chap. 15, pp. 611–668, wherein the discussion of the "New List" occupies pp. 645–662.

In 1904, Peirce made a proposal which, in advance, went to the heart of the semiological enterprise in all its post-Saussurean variants. Peirce noted that the investigation of signs will likely go nowhere if we make it depend on an arbitrary definition of sign stipulated as the model or paradigm for the whole study of signs. The question we must address, he said, is the question *what is a sign according to its being as a sign*, not merely according to our first impressions or particular interests, let alone our arbitrary stipulations.[12] And the only way to answer *this* question is by studying, not stipulating, what signs do within experience, 'common' (or cœnoscopic) or 'specialized' (ideoscopic) — by studying "how signs actually work"[13] in enabling us to reach and develop knowledge of objects.

Thus, where Saussure began with a *stipulated* definition arbitrarily restricting signs to the human sphere and severing their connection with the motivating history of the sign users as embodied in their language (the very "House of Being", as Heidegger well taught[14]), Peirce, exactly as Augustine at the first dawn of a prospect of a semiotic consciousness,[15] began with a *descriptive* definition based on observation rather than on a specialized and artificial analysis turning the study of signs into yet one more 'science' in the

---

[12] Peirce 1904: 8.322: "What is the essential difference between a sign that is communicated to a mind, and one that is not so communicated? If the question were simply what we *do* mean by a sign, it might soon be resolved. But that is not the point. We are in the situation of a zoölogist who wants to know what ought to be the meaning of "fish" in order to make fishes one of the great classes of vertebrates. It appears to me that the essential function of a sign is to render inefficient relations efficient — not to set them into action, but to establish a habit or general rule whereby they will act on occasion. ... A sign therefore is an object which is in relation to its object on the one hand and to an interpretant on the other, in such a way as to bring the interpretant into a relation to the object, corresponding to its own relation to the object."

[13] See, for example, "How do signs work?", in Deely 1994: 151–182.

[14] Heidegger 1947; see specific applications of this notion to the semiotic development in Deely 2000 and 2004.

[15] Deely 2009: 7–58, "The Initiation of Protosemiotics"; see Deely 2006c, where the first realization of the extent of Augustine's notion of *signa data* as including phytosemiosis is pinpointed in Augustine's Latin text.

very modern sense that the need for interdisciplinary approaches, already even in Saussure's time, was emerging as a reaction to. We consider anything to be a sign only when it stands for or represents something *other than itself* to some third thing (often, but not necessarily, a person); and it is quite obvious, cenoscopically as well as ideoscopically, that this relation of "one thing standing for another" can be observed to occur among all animals able to learn from experience, including therefore but illimitable to human animals. (This, indeed, later became Sebeok's own starting point for breaking through the artificial boundaries semiology worked so hard to establish and maintain in its futile effort to contain the study of signs within the perspectives and epistemological limits established for intellectual culture by modern philosophy.)

4.4. Protosemiotic Antecedents

Peirce differed from Saussure and the general run of modern intellectuals in yet another particular that proved important: he did not dismiss the pre-modern Latin scholastics out of hand (as Descartes had successfully urged), but studied them in considerable depth. It is not too much to say perhaps[16] that it was from those Latin studies modernity had begun by proscribing (as we saw above[17]) that Peirce acquired his appetite for the doctrine of signs — an appetite incompatible, as it proved, with modern philosophy, from its beginnings, yes, but *especially* after Kant. Not so much the details of modern philosophy as the fundamental epistemological orientation and conceptions regarding language and experience were the problem. But in the writings on sign of the later Latins Peirce found that his proposal for descriptively defining signs in terms of an irreducibly triadic relation was the very notion that the late Latins, in what can only be characterized historically as the first florescence of semiotic consciousness, had elaborated to the point of a *demonstrated fact*.

---

[16] Beuchot and Deely 1995.

[17] See the discussion of Descartes 1628, pp. 9–10 above.

So Peirce was able to realize early in his own development two crucial facts. First, that the actual being of a sign is not any one of the three terms related in an actual signification but the very *relation itself* that unites the three terms, exactly as the protosemioticians had determined.[18] Second, that what we call a "sign" in common usage is in fact not a sign strictly speaking but rather some particular being — whether external, as is a sound, mark, or movement; or internal, as is a psychological state, cognitive or cathectic — that happens to occupy the position of "standing for" in a triadic relation referring what is stood for as object to some third, this 'third' being most obviously a cognitive organism (human or not), Peirce allowed, but perhaps not necessarily so (hence his distinction between interpret*er* and interpret*ant* regarding this third term of the triad necessary for there to be the full relation constituting "sign" in its formal being); for we need to inquire at length into the manner in which signs function before we can justly assign limits to the extent or range of that action: a caution that goes to the heart of Sebeok's influence on the later semiotic developments.

4.5. The Being Proper to Signs

Since the sign consists in a relation (the *point d'accord* between Peirce and Saussure) which, like every relation triadic or not, is imperceptible and suprasubjective, and since (the point that quite escaped Saussure's notice, and scarred his heritage as modern rather than postmodern directly) the position of anything among the terms of this triad is what makes something we can see, hear, or point to be called 'a sign', it becomes clear at once that *actually anything* can *become* a sign, regardless of its subjective constitution.[19]

---

[18] Deely 2009: esp. Sections 9.1.–9.2, 67–74.

[19] Indeed, the Latins had already pointed out that while sign in general consists in a relation indifferently real or unreal ("ontological" in that sense: *relatio secundum esse* — See Poinsot 1632: Book I, Question 1, opening paragraphs), the whole difference between so-called natural signs, on the one hand, and together stipulated and customary signs, on the other hand (i.e., signs in the sense identified by Saussure as 'arbitrary'), lies precisely in the fact that subjective constitution as such

What is one time sign can be another time object, or even the one to or for which the object is represented. A 'sign' in the common sense is actually not a thing but a role.[20] Peirce proposed, accordingly, that, technically, it might be better to speak of 'representamens' (a less technically formidable proposal has been the expression 'sign-vehicle') than 'signs', calling then the represented 'the signified object' or 'significate',[21] and calling the third to or for whom the representamen represents its significate 'the interpretant' (and leaving open, as we noted, the question of whether the interpretant be mental).

So, in his descriptive and experimental approach to discovering the being proper to signs, you should *note that Peirce's idea of the significate is without counterpart in Saussure's scheme.* While Saussure's *signifiant* finds a counterpart in Peirce's representamen, and Saussure's *signifié* finds something of a counterpart in Peirce's interpretant,[22] Peirce's significate finds *no counterpart at all* in Saussure's model for sign.[23] This is not some minor inconvenience, but

---

enters into the proper signifying of the former but not the latter signs. Hence, by assimilating the account of natural signs to his stipulated paradigm, Saussure eliminated the zoösemiotic component of human communication in a manner exactly paralleling Descartes' elimination of animality from the essential definition of the human being.

[20] This was, in my opinion, the essential intuition behind Eco's attempt in 1976 to replace the notion of 'sign' with, rather, the notion of 'sign-function' — a proposal, nonetheless, later happily if silently abandoned: see Deely 2001: Chap. 16.

[21] This last term, "significate", being a word to which the makers of English dictionaries remain interestingly resistant to admitting into their vocabulary, patently incognizant of the fact that what "significate" says plainly and openly "object" says also but obscurely and in a hidden way: see the complete establishment of this point in Deely 2009a.

[22] I say "something of" a counterpart, rather than simply "a counterpart", because while the 'obvious' meaning of a significate (*signifié*) would be 'the thing signified', in Saussure's system the *signifié* is never a thing but rather an image or 'idea' in the mind of the speaker, a part of the language-user's subjectivity, as is indeed the interpretant in those not rare cases when it is 'something mental'. See Deely 2009d.

[23] The object presented in an anthroposemiosis for Peirce (or Poinsot) is never in direct awareness or speaking a subjective component of the speaker's mentality,

turns out to go the heart of the matter of how the study of signs ought to be named.

4.6. The Name "Semiotics"

It was Saussure's proposed model for the study of signs that "caught on" in the popular and academic intellectual culture of the early-to-mid-20th century throughout Europe and the Americas, but here we find also a curious divide. "Semiology" as the name Saussure proposed for this study was the name adopted throughout Western Europe and the Americas. But in Eastern Europe, in the development erstwhile known as "Soviet semiotics", even though there was universal acceptance of Saussure's dyadic model for the development, the Tartu-Moscow school preferred from the start the name "semiotics" as earlier proposed by Locke for the study in the conclusion of his 1690 *Essay*.

In the West, in sharp contrast with the Soviet/Tartu-Moscow development, "semiotics" was a marginal term adopted only by those who opposed the claim that Saussure's dyadic model of sign was an adequate basis for a general science or "doctrine" of signs (as it came also alternatively to be known[24]). The turning point in

---

but on the contrary something suprasubjective and public in principle, and this even when the object is not also a material thing. So if one uses Saussure's term *signifié* technically and correctly according to Saussure's specifications, then there is no Saussurean term to designate the object in the sign relation. But were one to go with the 'obvious meaning' of 'significate' by (mis)taking that term as Saussure's way of expressing a 'significate' in the sense of a thing sometimes independent of the speaker, then it would be the interpretant that is without counterpart in the Saussurean scheme. Either way, the triad of vehicle-object-interpretant of a signification is demolished when using the Saussurean model as a *patron général* for the analysis of language (or anything else in a culture). (The case is analogous in its power to mislead with the term "physical" in Brentano's "mental/physical" distinction, where the 'obvious' meaning of 'physical' is a material object of the external world, whereas in fact Brentano's own explanation of 'physical' rules out that 'obvious' construal as mistaken — see Reading 8 in Cobley ed. 2009.)

[24] Interestingly, the Latin expression, "doctrina signorum", turns out to be the oldest generic designation for sign-study, from Augustine's time to the work of Poinsot. Locke, in introducing his novel Greek spelling for the name that would be, via a Latin transliteration, "semiotics", expressly posed semiotics as synonymous

this matter turned out to be Sebeok's entry into the intellectual fray, particularly with his identification of the adoption of Saussure's notion of sign as a "pars pro toto" fallacy. By 20th century's end, "semiology" had all but completely been replaced in Western Europe and the Americas by the previously marginal term "semiotics" — to such an extent that those who insist on working within the strictures for sign that Saussure laid down with his proposal of his crippled linguistic sign as *le patron générale* for all sign studies have some explaining to do in calling themselves "semioticians", even with the cover provided by the history of the Tartu-Moscow school! For while a semiologist can indeed be a semiotician, he or she can hardly any longer claim to have a specialty or a viewpoint which provides the foundations for the whole of semiotics, any more than an astrologer these days (in contrast to the times of Galileo and Brahe) can lay claim to the science of astronomy.

So credit for the name "semiotics" as displacing "semiology" in the West goes above all to Sebeok; but credit for the name itself goes to Locke, from whom not only Lotman in the East but Peirce in the West seems to have taken this name for sign studies in general. At the conclusion of his *Essay* of 1690, Locke pointed out that all knowledge consists of awareness either of things which are as they are or of things as we are able to make them to be, but that in both cases it is in and through signs that the knowledge is reached in the first place, developed, or communicated. The study, then, of signs as the necessary instrument of *all* knowledge Locke proposed should be named with a derivation of the Greek term originally

---

with the expression "doctrine of signs", an expression also used by Peirce early on (hence the title for Colapietro and Olshewsky 1996, for example), and in the later 20th century opted for by Thomas A. Sebeok in preference to Saussure's expression "science of signs". The tapestry of this etymological history weaves throughout the 20th century developments of semiotics, particularly after Sebeok expressed his preference at the opening of his seminal volume of 1976, *Contributions to the Doctrine of Signs*. My own involvement in the weaving is consequent upon Sebeok's choice of the expression, and records close to the full history of the subsequent discussion: see Deely 1976, 1977, 1978, 1982a, 1985: esp. 414–417, 1986a, 1986b, 2004e, 2006a, 2006b; and Williams Deely 2010.

associated in ancient times with medicine and sailing especially,[25] a term which transliterates from Locke's text as what would be in Latin *semiotica*, or in English *semiotics*.

With the notable exception of Algirdas Greimas (1917–1992) and the so-called "Soviet Semiotics" of Eastern Europe, then, we may say that the thinkers of the later 20th century who adopted the name "semiotics" for the study of signs, instead of the heady and fashionable "semiology", tended to be precisely those who recognized the arbitrary and artificially restrictive stipulation of Saussure — Thomas A. Sebeok chief among them.[26] The initial preference outside the Soviet sphere of 20th century Eastern Europe for calling the study of signs "semiotics" rather than "semiology" was based firmly on the recognition of the Saussurean model of sign as flatly inadequate to encompass what common sense (more precisely: cenoscopic analysis!) immediately recognizes of the action of signs in experience and nature, and all the more so once the semiotic understanding of the triadic relation forming to make one thing represent another as object to another as subjected to an action of signs, or semiosis (as Peirce named the peculiar activity of renvoi manifesting the workings of a sign) has come into play.

At this juncture, the followers of Saussure have but two options. Like Tarasti, they can opt for the Way of Signs after all, incorporating Saussure's insights into semiotics by explicitly recognizing that the relation constitutive of sign is not dyadic but triadic (so that Saussure's *signifiant* and *signifié* cannot adequately be thought without the addition of the *significatum*). Or they can remain on the Way of Ideas, leaving out the *significatum* by insisting that only signs which fit Saussure's definition of arbitrariness really are signs, and that since (after all) there is really nothing in a name, it makes no difference whether you call the analysis based on Saussure's paradigm "semiotics"

---

[25] The work of Manetti remains the best survey of ancient thought in this matter, particularly — but not limited to — Manetti 1987 (in English 1993).

[26] See the details concerning Sebeok himself in Deely 2005b; and now in the much larger tribute volume *Semiotics Continues To Astonish* ..., ed. Paul Cobley, John Deely, Kalevi Kull, and Susan Petrilli (Berlin: Mouton de Gruyter, 2010).

or "semiology", since the fact remains that semiotics begins and ends with that part alone of Peirce's semiosis which human beings have in their conscious control. As between pragmaticism and pragmatism the dividing line is nominalism, so also between semiology as proposed by Saussure and the doctrine of signs as semiotics.

4.7. What's in a Name?

What is in a name, then? This is not a question the semiotician can afford to ignore, or to answer lightly.

For the anthropocentrism of modernity's *res cogitans* dies hard among those who have imbibed it through the cultural unconscious along with their mother's milk; and we see even today those clinging to the idealist, determinately modern perspective of semiology yet trying to pass themselves off as "semioticians" (even though they have embraced a methodology which blocks, arbitrarily and unwarrantably, the path of semiotic inquiry into nature as a larger whole).

It is not that semiology is inherently worthless and needs to be consigned, root and branch, to the ash heap of modern philosophy's idea of "epistemology". Not at all. Semiology, however, does need to drop all pretensions to being adequate to the full requirements of semiotic inquiry, and accept its subalternate status and role as a *pars semeioticae* within a larger whole — and hence above all to drop its pretense that there is "nothing in a name". Only by recognizing its modest place and finding ways to shed its arbitrary limitations in understanding that all signs, in culture or nature, are channels of communication, and not isolated features of the communicative process, will semiology in new forms survive the transition to postmodern times and find its own place within the semiotic consciousness of postmodern culture.

4.8. The Turning Point in the Development Overall

The decisive turning point in the modern development of the doctrine of signs as a systematic and thematic inquiry into the action of signs wherever that action is to be found (a matter which, as

I hope has become clear through the foregoing remarks, cannot be a-priori stipulated), no doubt came about principally through the interventions of Thomas A. Sebeok in the community of inquirers, beginning about 1963 with his introduction of zoösemiotics as a central notion.

By the 1980s, Sebeok had firmly distinguished between *semiotics* as the major tradition of inquiry into signs and *semiology* as a potentially legitimate subcurrent within the major tradition, but *minor*, even as human beings as part of larger nature are but a *small* part — "that minuscule part of nature that we grandiosely label culture", as Sebeok put it,[27] and to which the die-hard semiologists (under whatever name) would short-sightedly confine semiotic inquiry.

4.9. The Aim in the Present Work

The present essay has one single aim: to define the expression "semiotic animal" so as firmly to fix its usage once and for all, so far as possible, all within the contours of the major tradition of semiotics. This tradition, unlike its subalternate counterpart, semiology,[28] and like pragmaticism as Peirce contrasted it with pragmatism,[29] admits of no possibility of confinement to the modern mainstream with its nominalistic underpinnings and idealistic thrust. For semiotics enters the 21st century well-established around a firm core of 'scholastic realism', indeed, yet within a development of the doctrine of signs that moves beyond both idealism and realism in the modern sense to introduce the postmodern era of philosophy within an increasingly global intellectual culture.

---

[27] Sebeok 1984: 2; I paraphrase.

[28] Deely 1986a, and 2001: Chap. 16.

[29] See Deely 1999, and 2001: esp. 616ff.

Chapter 5

Etymological Tracings

In his article "Zoosemiotics" for *American Speech* 43.2 (May 1968), p. 144, Thomas A. Sebeok concluded as follows:

> Although the authorship of a handful of invented English words is known since the seventeenth century — for instance, of *gas, physicist* and *scientist, chortle, kodak,* and *blurb* — Hockett (1958: 393) justly observes that "we cannot usually know the exact identity of the innovating individual". If the innovating individual happens to be a linguist, he has an obligation, I think, to state the circumstances of his creation and to trace its history in the language and its spread, so far as he can, in other languages. Such has been my purpose in briefly presenting this five-year record of *zoosemiotics*.

What Sebeok says of the linguist applies no less to the semiotist as philosopher, particularly when it comes to something as important as our very understanding of our own being.

The earliest record we have of the expression "semiotic animal" occurs in 1897 in the German language, in a text of the prominent mathematician Felix Hausdorff (1868–1942), a man driven to suicide in order to escape the Nazi operations against Jews. The text in which he introduces, though only passingly,[1] the expression "semiotic animal", occurs in a book published under the *nom de plume* 'Paul Mongré': "Der Mensch ist ein semiotisches Thier" — "The human being is a semiotic animal".

The term then falls dormant a full eighty-one years, till it crops up again in 1978, this time in the Italian language, in a text by Ferrucio Rossi-Landi (1921–1985). Rossi-Landi's usage (1978: 217) is again but a passing one (occurring even slightly more passingly than Hausdorff's German usage, which at least gave us a thematic paragraph on the point): "L'uomo, quale animale semiotico, è semiotico per intero" — "The human being, as a semiotic animal, is semiotic through and through".

Yet another twelve years pass, but now in 1990 for the first time the expression begins to take on a thematic character, being introduced in the opening paragraph and again in the concluding paragraph (with a note in between)[2] of my book outlining the *Basics of Semiotics*, a book described by Thomas A. Sebeok at the time as "the only successful modern English introduction" to the subject precisely because it undertook to outline the full range prospective for discovering an action of signs, in contrast to arbitrarily stipulating where alone such action should be looked for. Independently again (though perhaps unconsciously from Rossi-Landi, inasmuch as she was involved with his work over many years) the term crops up again in Italian in a 1998 book by Susan Petrilli,[3] but again (in contrast with the passing use of Rossi-Landi) now too with strongly systematic overtones.

Each one of the three first known usages — the German of 1897, the Italian of 1978, the English of 1990 — amount to a coinage, in that they are proposed and arrived at in complete independence of one another. Indeed, the earliest Hausdorff usage was only discovered thanks to the involvement in the discussion of Jeff

---

[1]   Mongré 1897: ¶7, p. 7.

[2]   Deely 1990: 2, 24n7, 124.

[3]   Petrilli 1998: 3, 181–182.

Bernard, who provoked Frieder Nake, through an e-mail exchange on the matter in the closing months of 2004, to uncover the Hausdorff text, of which Deely was able to obtain from the storage facility of Rice University in Houston the only copy of the work in the whole of North America![4]

There is, however, this considerable difference in the original German coinage and the later coinages in Italian and English where the expression takes on thematic overtones within the semiotic development: Hausdorff explains his expression in the terms that would, by the mid-twentieth century, be associated mainly with the glottocentric minor tradition of semiotics commonly called "semiology":[5]

> The human being is a semiotic animal; the humanity of this animal consists in this, that instead of the natural expression of needs and satisfactions the human being has appropriated a conventional, symbolic, only mediately understandable 'speech in signs'. The semiotic animal pays for things according to a nominal value, ... the beast[6] ... in real values.

In the dominant intellectual climate of the idealism against which Peirce had just begun his struggle, such a manner of putting the matter is understandable, almost inevitable, but it remains marginal to the central development of semiotics itself as a *doctrina signorum*.

The much later usage of the expression in question in works of Deely and Petrilli have in common firm roots in the major tradition of semiotics which traces its immediate lineage to Sebeok as well as Peirce, and thence back through Poinsot, the Conimbricenses, Soto, Scotus, Roger Bacon and Aquinas to Augustine. In this

---

[4] As a result, a bound photocopy now also exists in Deely's personal library at the University of St. Thomas, Houston.

[5] Mongré 1897: 7, ¶7: "Der Mensch ist ein semiotisches Thier; seine Menschheit besteht darin, dass er statt des natürlichen Ausdrucks seiner Bedürfnisse und Befriedigungen sich eine conventionelle, symbolische, nur mittelbar verständliche Zeichensprache angeeignet hat. Er zahlt in Nominalwerthen, ... Thier ... in Realwerthen."

[6] "Beast": see Section 7.1. (p. 40 below) on this contrast of *animalia rationalia* to the *animalia bruta*.

tradition, the oppositional sense of the worlds of "nature" vs. "culture" is rejected in favor of seeing cultural creation itself as a natural extension of the activities of the semiotic animal according to what is proper to it as a part of nature — a "participant observer",[7] not an "outside observer" as modern philosophy (and even modern science to some extent) imagined. As earlier work well showed,[8] with respect to the major tradition of semiotics semiology is but *that part* of the study of the action of signs limited to the species-specifically human world (as if spiders were to consider all other animals as not truly involved in the action of signs on the grounds that the others do not spin webs) as under some measure of voluntary control:[9]

> For if the *anthropos* as semiotic animal is an interpretant of semiosis in nature and culture alike, that can only be because the ideas of this animal, in their function as signs, are not limited to either order, but have rather, as we explained above, the universe in its totality — "all that wider universe, embracing the universe of existents as a part" — as their object.

Indeed, with Petrilli, the coinage is intended to open the way for developing the specifically semiotic dimension of ethical or moral consciousness in the human animal:[10]

---

[7] See T. von Uexküll 1982; Williams 1982.

[8] See Deely, Williams, and Kruse eds. 1986; Baer 1977, 1992.

[9] Deely 1990: 124.

[10] Petrilli 1998: 182. Earlier (p. 8), distinguishing between semiotics as the *study* of the action of signs and the *action of signs itself* (or semiosis) as the object of study, Petrilli proposes to call "metasemiosis" the realization in consciousness 'that there are signs', a realization which occurs and can only occur specifically within that general region of the action of signs we call anthroposemiosis.

This terminology, on first hearing (as I have discussed at more length in Deely 2009: Section 14.5., pp. 197–199), seemed to me somewhat unfortunate, inasmuch as I took it to reflect the unhealthy dominance in 20th century analytic philosophy (as also in semiology as an idealist strain from linguistics) of a view of language as an autonomous realm that can be treated as if it were independent of the deeper semioses of animal life and nature in general. A terminology that is reflective within semiotics of a 'philosophy of language' that is incompatible with the major tradition of semiotics as the doctrine of signs leading "everywhere in nature, including [into] those domains where humans have never set foot" (Emmeche 1994:

semiotics ... belongs to neither this nor that ideology, but concerns the *prise de conscience* and consequent behavioral responsibility of the human being as a "semiotic animal" for semiosis over the entire planet.

And in later writing, Petrilli, together with Augusto Ponzio, will propose the felicitous name for this new development: *semioethics*,[11] certainly one of the most important areas of semiotic development today.[12]

---

126) is hardly a terminology to be embraced, particularly by such distinguished authors as Petrilli and Ponzio who (e.g., 2001) have shown themselves well aware of and central contributors to the major tradition of "global semiotics" (as they characterize it by preference).

Yet this first impression misled me, for there is actually no reflection at all of analytic so-called "philosophy of language" in the term metasemiosis as Petrilli and Ponzio proposed it. Within the major tradition, that specific development of anthroposemiosis — in contrast with anthroposemiosis as such and as a whole — wherein the human animal begins to thematize the awareness of signs as such and their universal role in knowledge and experience, resulting in precisely the doctrine of signs or "semiotics" (as the study of organisms results precisely in that body of knowledge we call "biology"), may certainly with justice be termed a "metasemiosis", as long as we well understand the uselessness (not to say groundlessness) of going on to speak of a "metasemiotics", which would be a 'joining of what are unsuited to be joined', a *contradictio in adiectis*. In this more restricted and very specific sense, as a synonym for "semiotics" as the knowledge consequent upon thematizing the action of signs, we may well speak of a "metasemiosis". For anthroposemiosis has proceeded in the main with that typical animal oblivion to the being proper to signs (otherwise, semiotics as a modality or form of human awareness would have blossomed long before late modernity!); and when, within anthroposemiosis, the action and being proper to signs does finally begin to be thematized, we do indeed move to the level of a veritable "metasemiosis", and this is the level of semiotics itself as the doctrine of signs beyond the frontiers of the modern opposition of "idealism" to "realism" within philosophical tradition.

[11] Petrilli and Ponzio 2003, 2009. See also Petrilli 2003; Petrilli and Ponzio 2004; Deely 2004a. See the concluding paragraph of Chapter 9, p. 79 below, and p. 80n7.

[12] Eero Tarasti (2000), for example, under the title of *Existential Semiotics*, points to the need for this development, but without managing to suggest a nomenclature directly expressing the distinctively semiotic cast required for the enterprise of rethinking ethics in the context of a "semiosphere" which englobes the biological no less than the culture. By contrast, Tarasti's terminology hearkens back rather to the phenomenology and existentialism of mid-20th century late modern intellectual culture, when "semiologists" were still caught up in their *pars pro toto* fallacy.

Chapter 6

A "Catholic Preamble"[1]

The modern era opened under the sign of the *res cogitans*, the thinking thing, proposed by Descartes as the definition to replace the presuppositioned classical definition of human being as a "rational animal". From the point of view of Thomistic philosophy in the early modern period, this modern proposal for the understanding of the human being left much to be desired; but the heady currents of the modern mainstream carried all before it for the next three centuries and more.

The 2003 Thomistic Congress to consider humanism as we enter the third Christian millennium,[2] convened at the behest of Pope John Paul II, needs to be seen against the backdrop of this same Pope's earlier encyclical[3] on the relations of faith and reason,

---

[1] The term "Catholic" here means neither "theological" nor "religious in a sectarian sense", but refers to that broad spectrum of writings which, through reflection upon and in continuity with the medieval Latin heritage of thought, have contributed to the development of the understanding of contemporary problems as those problems are articulations of experience brought to linguistic expression. This sense of the term is discussed at length in Deely 1997.

[2] International Congress on "Christian Humanism in the Third Millennium: The Perspective of Thomas Aquinas", Rome, 21–25 September 2003.

[3] Wojtyła 1998, "Fides et Ratio".

wherein he noted[4] that, as the third millennium opens, our age has been termed by increasingly many "the age of 'postmodernity'." This term, the Pope goes on to say, "designates the emergence of a complex of new factors which, widespread and powerful as they are, have shown themselves able to produce important and lasting changes". But it is also a term that, as "transposed into the philosophical field", has "remained somewhat ambiguous", even though "one thing however is certain": namely, that, on the one hand, "the currents of thought which claim to be postmodern merit appropriate attention"; and, on the other hand, the final evaluation of these currents depends largely "on the delicate question of the demarcation of the different historical periods".

This problem singled out by the Pope of the demarcation of the historical epochs of philosophy, precisely for the purpose of establishing a standpoint from which the ambiguity surrounding the meaning of "postmodern" for philosophy might be reduced or eliminated, and from which a judgment on what is positive and what is negative in the designation of the term "postmodern" might be reached, in fact has been recently addressed in a large book.[5] Here my intention is to address just one limited — but decisive — consequence of that re-evaluation of modernity and its relation to

---

[4] Ibid., ¶91: "A quibusdam subtilioribus auctoribus aetas nostra uti tempus 'post-modernum' est designata. Ita verbum idem … in provinciam deinde philosophiae est translatum, at certa semper ambiguitate signatum, tum quia iudicium de iis quae uti 'post-moderna' appellantur nunc affirmans nunc negans esse potest, tum quia nulla est consensio in perdifficili quaestione de variarum aetatum historicarum terminis." — "Our age has been termed by some thinkers the age of 'postmodernity'. The term … was finally transposed into the philosophical field, but has remained somewhat ambiguous, both because judgment on what is called 'postmodern' is sometimes positive and sometimes negative, and because there is as yet no consensus on the delicate question of the demarcation of the different historical periods."

Wojtyła's last point is precisely that raised by Schmitz 1990: 153–54: "in determining the meaning of post-modernity, when is modernity supposed to have ended? … And in what is modernity supposed to have consisted? These questions are of decisive importance since the meaning given to the term 'post-modernity' is parasitic upon the meaning given to the term 'modernity'."

[5] See Deely 2001: 589.

the previous epochs of philosophy, namely, the manner in which a postmodern formulation of what distinguishes human understanding suggests also the requirement of a new definition of human being, one that will supersede the *res cogitans* even as the *res cogitans* superseded the "rational animal" (and modernity superseded the Latin Age beloved of medievalists everywhere).

Chapter 7

A Semiotic Reading of the History of Philosophy

Unfortunately, there is much, too much, that has simply to be presupposed in such a limited venue as the one in which we have here to operate. So, cutting to the chase, let me starkly state that the postmodern era, as stated above, opened with Charles Sanders Peirce clearing away of the underbrush to reveal from the work of his Latin predecessors in semiotics[1] a "way of signs", running from Augustine through Aquinas and down to the end of the Latin Age[2] in the synthesizing work of John Poinsot, contemporary of Galileo and Descartes.

This way of signs alone actually establishes the contacts and dependencies between human thought and action, on the one side, and the physical universe surrounding us as context for that thought

---

[1] The reader who wants the references and details of Peirce's dependency in his semiotic upon the late Latin medieval development can consult Beuchot and Deely 1995. See also Deely 2001: Chapter 15; Deely 2009 for the protosemiotic development.

[2] Again we have the matter of a story not well known among English-speaking philosophers. Details of this Latin "way of signs" are best found in the numerous writings of the Mexican philosopher and scholar, Mauricio Beuchot 1980, 1983, 1986, 1987, 1991, 1993, 1995, 1998; and Beuchot ed. 1995. The only serious discussion of this path so far in English is Deely 2001: Part II, Chapters 8–11, and Part IV, Chapter 15; and now also 2008b (for the transition from Latin to the national languages in early modern philosophy) and 2009 (for the original Latin florescence of semiotics, so-called "protosemiotics"). A volume *Redefining Medieval Philosophy* should be out in 2010.

and action, while at the same time accounting for the realization so dear to the moderns and (indeed!) at the heart of modernity so far as concerns science and philosophy, the place for a social construction of reality as part and parcel of human experience.[3] The discovery of what is distinctively human in the action of signs, it turns out, displaces Descartes' notion of the isolated thinker with a contextualized animal whose behavior is distinctive in the realization that there are signs[4] upon which the *whole of life* depends for successful continuance.

Since the knowledge that arises from this realization of the role of signs is called "semiotics", we will see that the definition of the human being as "semiotic animal" best captures and expresses the understanding of human beings that corresponds to the exploration of the "way of signs", the postmodern path of understanding the web of human experience as not subjectively isolated from but inextricably entangled with the physical universe. The problem is no longer the modern one of overcoming the isolation of the human species, but of revealing intelligently the tangle of dependencies, the semiotic web (as Sebeok called it[5]) which interrelates the human species with the larger universe in and from which the human species evolves.

This adventure of ideas marks an era in philosophy as much in contrast with modernity as modernity was in contrast with medieval (i.e., Latin) times.

7.1. Ancient and Medieval Philosophy

The philosophy of Greek and of Latin times was generally "realistic" in thinking that we can know what exists as it exists. Augustinian Neoplatonism, for example, did not differ from Aristotelian Thomism in the high middle age about *whether* we can come to

---

[3] See Deely 2005f.

[4] Without the formula "semiotic animal", the first formulation of this distinctive realization that I know of is to be found in Maritain 1956/1957 (definitive text published in Deely, Williams, and Kruse eds. 1986: 49–60).

[5] Sebeok 1975.

know reality in its independent being, but only concerning *what* that independent reality ultimately is and implies for human beings. Like the ancient Greeks before them, the medieval Latins always supposed they were on the "way of things" as they really are, whatever mistakes might befall along that way.[6] They never got so far as fully to distinguish thematically between *objects*, existing as such only in knowledge, and *things*, existing whether or not known. The understanding of the human being that accompanied this orientation, at least from the time of Porphyry (c.271AD), was expressed in the formula "rational animal" (*animal rationale*). Aristotle's own earlier formula (i.348/334BC) had been simply "linguistic animal", ζῷον λογον ἐχων, in contrast to the ζῷα λοφον ουκ ἐωων or "nonlinguistic animals" of Aristotle, the *animalia bruta* of the Latins.

7.2. Modern Philosophy

Modern philosophy came to an understanding of the difference between objects existing in knowledge and things existing independently of knowledge, but at the price of failing to show how things can themselves become objects. Where objects were mainly things for the earlier realisms, objects were mainly distinct from things for the early moderns. The connection between objects as what is known and things as existing became the nub of the issue. What was still mainly problematic in the modern mainstream after Descartes and Locke[7] became actually dogmatic in the synthesizing

---

[6] The way is well described, I think, in Deely 2001: both in Part I, and further in the subsection of Chap. 7, "The 'Way of Things', the Philosophy of Being, and Single-Issue Thomism", pp. 357–358.

[7] That monads, Leibniz's term for our thinking selves, "have no windows" was not the hard saying for the early moderns that it came to seem in late modernity. Still less had this view the character of a sophism too clever by half, as it appears in a postmodern light. Leibniz, indeed, spoke for the mainstream modern development when he adopted this view as the essence of his monadology, that little work which was itself the quintessence and summary modern statement about the nature of reality. What we call the physical universe is simply the totality of windowless monads, each locked in the living theater of its own representations.

But the moment people began to thematize their experience of communication and to think of communication as such as something real, the moment they

work of Kant identifying "the unknowable" through his twin (often crudely conflated[8]) distinctions between *Ding an sich*, on the side of the sensible aspect of objects, and *Noumenon*, on the side of the intelligible aspect of objects.[9] The understanding of human

---

began to think of *that* experience as a proper starting point for philosophy, the days of modern philosophy were numbered. For with the substitution of the experience of communication for private ideas as the point of departure for considering "the nature and extent of humane understanding", with a belief in the occasional success of communication as the guiding notion for developing the consequences of that point of departure, postmodernism had begun.

[8]   See Deely 2001: 558–559.

[9]   The doctrine of "the unknowable" in Kant is best contrasted with what, according to Aquinas, is "unknowable" for the human mind. A good start toward a systematic exposition of this contrast can be found with the entry UNKNOWABILITY in the Index to Deely 2001: 1009. Modern students of Kant, generally preferring the trees to the forest, turn somersaults to avoid facing head-on the consequent that what Kant has rejected in his "epistemology" is *the whole tradition of natural philosophy from Aristotle's day to his own*. Schrader (1967: 188) among the endless series of Kantian commentators stands out quite rightly in stating outright that Kantian epistemology "cuts the nerve of philosophical inquiry"; but this relentless consequence (so firmly asserted early-on by Hegel) is what the Kantians go to no end of verbiage to conceal from themselves.

What Aristotle called ον and the Latins called *ens reale* they deemed knowable antecedently to mind's activity and categorized it accordingly. Over against *ens reale* the Latins set *ens rationis*, also knowable but only consequent upon and produced by the mind's activity. The Kantian move could hardly have been more opposed to ancient and medieval thought alike, amounting to its *wholesale rejection*, in fact. For Kant set this ancient notion of *ens reale* over against the "appearances" of experience, and categorized it as an *empty unknowable*, the realm of the *Ding an sich*, "thing in itself". This "cutting of the nerve of inquiry" ought to be (again as Hegel urged) grounds by itself for relegation of the "critical philosophy" in which modernity culminated to the museum for the history of discredited notions — right up there alongside the proofs that flying machines are impossible or that the human body would fly apart if subjected to speeds above sixty miles per hour.

Hegel, alone among the influential mainstream moderns, goes for Kant's jugular in exposing the contradiction in asserting that we can know *that* something is but can in no way develop this initial knowledge. Yet in thinking that an ideal categorial scheme will enable us to arrive at the details of nature by principally deductive thought, even Hegel has still one foot in the way of ideas. Deely 2001: Chap. 13, discusses all of this in considerable detail. Here let Charles Peirce's summary suffice, from his "Lessons from the history of philosophy" (1903: CP 1.19): "Kant was a nominalist; ... Hegel was a nominalist of realistic yearnings. ... In one word, all modern philosophy of every sect has been nominalistic."

being that accompanied the modern divorce of objects from things came thus to be enshrined in the original formula "thinking thing" (*res cogitans*) proposed at modernity's dawn.

7.3. Transition to Semiotics: a Postmodern Era Opens in Philosophy

Philosophy became *"postmodern"*, then, when the work of Charles S. Peirce recovered and advanced the original semiotic consciousness of the Latin Age. That consciousness, initiated by Augustine's first crude notion of "sign in general",[10] was finally systematized in the 17th century work of John Poinsot,[11] that careful follower of St. Thomas Aquinas who wrote in Latin under the name *Joannes a Sancto Thoma*[12] and who became, in the twentieth century, alongside St. Thomas himself, the principal teacher of Jacques and Raïssa Maritain. Maritain deemed Poinsot the last and greatest of the geniuses who had advanced Thomistic thought in the Latin line. Be that as it may, our interest is that with the retrieval and thematic development by Peirce of the original semiotic consciousness developed among the Latins,[13] it became possible to understand how, through the action of signs, objects and things are interwoven in the fabric of human experience in a manner that transcends the modern opposition of idealism to realism.

The argument to be advanced here is that understanding of human being that develops from within and together with this postmodern perspective is precisely captured in the formula "semiotic animal" (*animal semeioticum*), a formula that is no mere

---

This was also why, in the end, Peirce felt it necessary to distinguish *pragmaticism* from *pragmatism*, the former being incompatible with all forms of nominalism (another discrimination students of American thought strive mightily not to face up to). Consult the website maintained by The Metaphysical Club at the University of Helsinki, especially *The Red Book* and *The Green Book* (Deely 1991), at <http://www.helsinki.fi/science/commens/papers.html>.

[10] See Deely 1998 and 2006c.

[11] Deely 1998a and 2009.

[12] See, in Deely 1985: EA II, "The Author of the Treatise", A., "Name and National Origin", 421–424.

[13] See Deely 1998b and 2006, and Beuchot and Deely 1995.

approximative description, as it turns out, but an expression that is actually definitional, i.e., one that applies to *all and only* human beings among the terrestrial animal organisms. For "semiotic animal", unlike prima facie kindred expressions such as "signifying animal",[14] or "symbolic animal",[15] identifies what is without qualification the species-specific case of human being, whereas these other formulae taken alone suffer the logical deficiency of being "too broad", that is to say, of including *more animals than* only semiotic animals. Let us examine the prima facie alternatives, one by one.

7.3.1. In search of a definition of the human: why not "signifying animal"?

When we say that the human being is "a signifying animal", we are saying something true indeed but true of every animal that has ever lived or ever will live. The human being is a signifying animal, but so is the hawk, crow, dog, alligator, centipede, termite, etc. In applying the expression to human animals, further qualification is necessary to show what is distinctive about the signifying in the human case.

7.3.2. In search of a definition of the human: why not "symbolic animal"?

The same — being a formula too broad — is true, albeit less obviously, when we say that the human being is "a symbolic animal". Yet this formula "symbolic animal" is capable of being understood in ways the are incompatible with the doctrine of signs, for example, when "symbolic" is understood in the context of or consistent with the modern epistemologies which proscribe knowledge of things in themselves — precisely where natural signs, σημεία, point the human understanding. And even when it is understood in quite "realistic terms" and in scientific contexts which quite successfully flout the limits posted for human knowing by the modern

---

[14] Rauch and Carr eds. 1980.

[15] Cassirer 1944, Deacon 1997.

philosophers who see only constructs, constructs, everywhere, with no way to pierce the phenomenal veil,[16] the expression "symbolic animal" or "symbolic species" cannot be restricted to the case of human animals without further explanation of what is distinctive of symbols in the human use of signs.

Thus, in the late modern twilight, one of Kant's interpreters, Ernst Cassirer, proposed *animal symbolicum* as an updated definition of the human being,[17] and Frieder Nake is far from alone in thinking that this Cassirean formula anticipates and is perhaps synonymous with the expression "semiotic animal", so the inadequacy of the Saussurean formula in providing basis for a definition of human being — let alone a postmodern definition — deserves some emphasis, for the excellent reason that a true definition and the reality defined must be co-extensive. The definition proposed, in order really to be a definition, must be, in the classical formula, "neither too broad nor too narrow".

Within semiotics, the point I am making is in fact no more than a reiteration of the point as made authoritatively by Thomas A. Sebeok at least as early as 1975 (1975a: 89):

> The fondly cherished mythic characterization of man adhered to by E. Cassirer's epigones and many others, as a unique *animal symbolicum* can be sustained only if the definition of 'sym-

---

[16] By reason only of a double failure of the modern philosophers is this "phenomenal veil" mistakenly deemed "unpiercable". There is the failure, first, to distinguish prescissively between sensation, on the one hand, and perception and intellection alike, on the other hand (in that the former does not while the latter do require a mental representation produced by the organism itself out of its own resources in response to some specifying stimulation). Second is the failure to recognize within sensation the semiotic character of the relations among so-called sense data which are never "atomic" but always semiosic and presented within a naturally determined network of objectifying relations reflective of the interacting subjectivity of environmental things with the subjectivity of the thing which the organism sensing is. See the "Sensory Manifold" diagram in Deely 1982: 114, 2008: 89, or 2009: 123.

[17] Cassirer 1944: 26: "instead of defining man as an *animal rationale* we should define him as an *animal symbolicum*. By so doing we can designate his specific difference, and we can understand the new way open to man — the way to civilization."

bol' is impermissibly ensnared with the concept of natural language . .... By every other definition — invoking the principle of arbitrariness, the idea of a conventional link between a signifier and its denotata, Peirce's 'imputed character', or the notion of an intensional class for the designatum — animals [other than human animals] demonstrably employ symbols.

Or again (1975b: 137):

Symbols are often asserted to be the exclusive property of man, the *animal symbolicum*, but the capacity of organisms to form intensional class concepts obtains far down in phylogenesis, and this ability for constructing universals from particulars was provided with a solid mathematical-neurological rationalization over a quarter of a century ago (Pitts and McCulloch 1947; cf. Arbib 1971). Both according to the definition of symbol offered in 5.1 [the reference is to a section on preceding page 134 of this same essay: "*A Sign* without either similarity or contiguity, but only *with a conventional link between its signifier and its denotata, and with an intensional class for its designatum, is called a symbol*"], and the more common Aristotelian definitions resting on the doctrine of arbitrariness that were promoted in linguistics especially by William Dwight Whitney and, after him, Saussure (Engler 1962; Coseriu 1967), animals undoubtedly do have symbols.

Sebeok's conclusion in brushing aside the neo-Kantian proposals may seem brusque, but the point is that it is *warranted and crucial* to the semiotic understanding of what human beings as animals are and are not. If "an unjustifiably excessive generalization and overly broad application of the concept of symbolic forms marks the writings of many of Ernst Cassirer's epigones or of those indirectly influenced by his philosophy",[18] all the more important is it that semiotics, which has as its task, after all, the understanding of semiosis, clarify the situation and rectify the terms involved. It is not tolerable for distinguished scholars such as, for example, Stanley

---

[18] Sebeok 1975b: 135.

Jaki,[19] to be influencing their students with such semiotically ig-norant assertions as that "Man is a symbol-making animal, and the only such animal known." For, in short, while human beings are the only animals capable of thematizing signs, they are far from the only animals that employ symbols.

So in fact there is nothing whatever postmodern, nor even distinctively semiotic, about the proposal that "man is a symbolic animal" or, as Deacon would generalize the proposal, a "symbolic species" (though Deacon is surely right in underlining the spe-cies-specific symbolicity at work in linguistic communication as it bears upon the biological aspects of human evolution). Further in fact, such a proposal is not even late or ultra-modern, but early to mid-modern, since we find it originally proposed already by Giambatista Vico (1668–1744)[20] in the development of the main-stream modern line which Kant would systematize by absolutiz-ing the φυσις/νομος (nature/culture) opposition as the sphere, respectively, of unknowable/knowable. The over-riding point for the present discussion, however, lies not in the dating but in the content of the expression: semiotics knows many uses of symbols among animals which are not human animals.[21] To call the human being a "symbolic animal", thus, is generic, but not, as a definition is required to be, species-specifically human. All animals signify, many animals make symbols, but only human animals are capable of de-veloping semiotics.

7.3.3. In search of a definition of the human: why not "linguistic animal"?

Linguistic communication is a species-specifically human mo-dality. It is also intrinsically semiotic. Why not then settle for calling

---

[19] Jaki 1999: 129.

[20] See Trabant 2004: Chapter 3.

[21] For more particulars on the occurrence of symbolic forms and usage beyond the human realm, see esp. Sebeok 1979; or (my two favorites) Kessel 1955, and von Frisch 1967. Needless to say, I am here pointing out, not exhausting, the literature on this important point.

human beings in the postmodern context "linguistic animal"? Surely this is not "too broad", and neither is it too narrow, for it includes all and only human beings?

And yet it is too narrow, for linguistic communication is only one of the many forms of semiosis in which the human animal engages, even if it is the most distinctive one in that it provides the interface that is necessary even if not sufficient for creating or entering into the realm of culture on the terms proper to anthropo-semiosis, as I have showed elsewhere at length.[22] Thus there can be a "metalinguistics", but a "metasemiotics" is utter nonsense, a "joining of unjoinables" or *contradictio in adiectis*, for semiotics is the study of the action of signs, all signs, among which language falls as a species-specific variety (and far from the only one when we extend our purview to zoösemiosis). Semiotics, thus, is *itself already* a "metase-miosis", as we noted earlier,[23] *and the whole of it*; while human language (linguistic communication, to be more precise), including its species-specifically distinctive metalinguistic considerations and maneuvers — contemporary "philosophy of language", in short[24] — falls under the genus of semiosis as but one of its subspecies, one part of that whole which semiotics takes as its distinctive proper object.

Thus, oddly enough, to define the human being as the "linguistic animal" says something true but yet something which, from a semiotic point of view, is too narrow. For it is still a formula in the tradition of *res cogitans*, seeing the human animal as above or cut off from the rest of nature, or at least as isolated within the animal kingdom by this unique communicative modality. By contrast, semiotics sees the isolated aspect of language as something true of every species-specific semiosis, something with which the animal kingdom (not to mention the plant kingdom) is replete, but further places these "isolating" semioses in continuity with *other* semioses which are essential even though in some sense external to the

---

[22] Notably Deely 1980, and 1982: Part II.

[23] See p. 32 above, footnote 10.

[24] See Deely 2006b, and 2009: 187–199.

species-specific semioses, as providing the necessary materials and contexts without which the species-specific semioses would falter and collapse — or implode.

I cannot say this better than Tzvetan Todorov put it some years ago:[25]

> As long as one questions oneself only on verbal language, one remains within a science (or a philosophy) of language. Only the breaking up of the linguistic framework justifies the founding of semiotics ... where words only occupy a place among other signs.

7.3.4. In search of a definition of the human: first some necessary preliminaries

The situation can only be clarified if, from early in the game, we can give a distinctive focus to what is truly postmodern about the understanding of the human situation that the way of signs involves for its explorers. And this clarification precisely is what the definitional formula "semiotic animal" is suited to point us toward, though we need more preliminaries before we fully can bring this fact to light. Let us try, then, to put just those needed preliminaries into play.

"Semiotics" is a word that is only beginning to be recognized in its theoretical importance for the nascent globality of postmodern intellectual culture.[26] The developing body of knowledge that semiotics names began to be thematized and organized as a field of investigation only in the later decades of the 20th century: sem-

---

[25] Todorov 1977: 40–41. For extended discussion of Todorov's point, see Deely 2006b.

[26] The first important survey of this word as a twentieth-century phenomenon was undertaken by Sebeok (1971). Detailed investigation into the contemporary provenance of the term "semiotics" was outlined by Sebeok in 1991, while something like a definitive inquiry was undertaken by Deely in an essay (2003d) that was chosen for the Mouton d'Or Award by an international jury of Frederik Stjernfelt, Denmark; Lúcia Santaella, Brazil; and Frank Nuessel, USA. This essay has since been published with additional materials as *Why Semiotics?* (Deely 2004).

iotics is the knowledge that arises from the study of the action of signs, called "semiosis" (first by Peirce). So "semiotics" names the knowledge that corresponds to the awareness and study of semiosis. The basic ideas in this area were heavily influenced by late Latin thinkers, in particular Duns Scotus (c.1266–1308) and the Conimbricenses (1607),[27] who in turn, were teachers of the first thinker to systematize the foundations of semiotics as a prospectively unified field for systematic investigation in his *Treatise on Signs* of 1632.

Even though Poinsot and not Peirce was the first systematically to establish the foundations of semiotics as a distinct subject matter focused prescissively on the triadic relation as providing for signs their formal or "proper" (i.e., distinctive) being, it remains that the role of the action of signs in the developing and sustaining of the fabric of human experience, both collective and individual, has only gradually made its way to the foreground of scientific and philosophical inquiry, and under the influence of Peirce above all in shifting the emphasis from the being to the action of signs.[28] As late as 1991, Sebeok was still struggling to make clear "the fact, not then self-evident" — as by 2001 the fact in question had, for many, finally become[29] — "that each and every man, woman, and child

---

[27] This seminal work, Conimbricenses 1606/7, the link between Peirce and Poinsot, has been published in bilingual form by Doyle 2001.

[28] See Deely 1988.

[29] The medieval Latins commonly distinguished two kinds of propositions under the heading of "self-evident" (*per se nota* or *selbstverständlichkeit*), namely, those self-evident to anyone understanding the immediate sense of the terms themselves from which the proposition is formed (*propositiones per se nota quoad omnes*), and those self-evident only "to the wise", i.e., to those who understand not merely the terms as such but the further implications that follow from their arrangement in this particular proposition, who have achieved a grasp of the larger context of intelligibility within which the proposition in question is able to maintain its sense (*propositiones per se nota quoad sapientes*). Sebeok is saying, by way of Introduction to the final book completed within his lifetime, that the proposition that human experience throughout is an irreducible, labile interweave of sign-relations both mind-dependent and mind-independent, is a proposition that has become self-evident within semiotics by the time we have entered the twenty-first century, a *propositio per se nota quoad sapientes*, something self-evident to semioticians insofar as they have come to understand that the being proper to signs consists in triadic

superintends over a partially shared pool of signs in which that same monadic being is immersed and must navigate for survival throughout its singular life."[30]

Hence, not surprisingly, the seminal work of Poinsot in demonstrating the importance for philosophy of a perspective which transcends the modern struggle between idealism and realism was lost to history, as it were, a vain anticipation of the further horizon of a postmodern intellectual culture and epoch that modernity, in philosophy's unfolding history, would, by its struggle with the opposition of "idealism" to "realism", define and show the need for. The role of the action of signs in the developing and sustaining of the fabric of human experience, both collective and individual, thus, has only gradually made its way to the foreground of scientific and philosophical inquiry. We are, in this matter, roughly at the stage of modern thought at the time of the publication of Galileo's 1632 *Dialogue concerning the Two Chief World Systems*. At that time, the Latin Age of scholasticism seemed to be in full bloom and ascendancy, but in fact something radically new was aborning, and "modernity" with its establishment of science in the modern sense ("ideoscopic" as opposed to "cœnoscopic" knowledge, as we would say[31]), was the light to the future.

That future is not only upon us, it has been upon us for some time. Modernity reached its zenith, not its beginning,[32] as the 18th century turned into the 19th; and by the time that century of modernity's full bloom and ascendancy drew to a close, again something radically new, all unnoticed, was aborning — to wit, a *postmodern* turn of intellectual culture restoring to the *res cogitans* not merely

---

relations indifferently real and unreal according to circumstance, but suprasubjective as relations in every case.

[30] Sebeok 2001: "Introduction", p. ix.

[31] See the Index entries on this cœnoscopic/ideoscopic distinction in Deely 2001: 865 and 910; and the full-blown discussion of the distinction now in Deely 2008, with further points in 2009e concerning the state of biosemiotics as the 21st century enters its second decade.

[32] See Santaella-Braga 1994.

its animality, but also its uniqueness *among* the animals. It was no longer a question of *reason* as the distinguishing mark, as it had been for the ancient *animal rationale* and the modern *res cogitans* alike, but something much broader, in which reason only participated in a distinctive way, something that linked the human self directly to the broader universe of nature not only animal but plant and purely physical as well. That something was the finally recognized *action of signs*, termed c.1883 "semiosis".[33]

---

[33] The coinage was by Charles Peirce, based on a reading and discussion of Philodemus i.54/40BC: see Fisch 1986. See further Manetti 1987/1993.

Chapter 8

Re-Evaluating the Relative

Now the most remarkable thing about this finally recognized distinctive action that makes the presence of signs known was the typical structure of being that it consequently revealed. As biology is the science that arises from the study of the action of living things, so (gradually over the 20th century, particularly in its final quarter) the knowledge that arises from the study of the action of signs (or semiosis) came to be called "semiotics".

But the "being" revealed by the action of signs turned out to be something that could not exactly be pointed to, the way one can point to the heart or the lungs of a living organism. Worse than that, the being distinctive of sign as sign turned out to be something that could neither be seen nor heard nor touched, nor indeed perceived directly by any of the senses, external or internal. The being distinctive of sign and constitutive of it *as* sign turned out to be a singular exemplification of relation itself, exactly as the protosemiotic development had been forced to conclude, "relation according to the way relation has its proper being as suprasubjective" (generally *relatio secundum esse* in the Latin Age after Boethius), irreducible to the inherent being of subjectivity ("*esse in*") as also to the being of intersubjectivity (*esse ad* in the categories of Aristotle).

Relation as suprasubjective in the structure of experience proved to be the most elusive of all the ways of being, often not recognized at all in earlier periods of philosophy as an element of *ens reale* in its own right, notably after Ockham's attempt to reduce relation as intersubjectivity to the mere multiplication of subjective similarities within ("*esse in*" or "*inesse*") individuals.[1] Among the Latins, emphasizing as they did 'reality' in its most hardcore sense, even those who did recognize the proper reality of relation[2] qualified it as "ens minimum" by comparison with substance and the inherent accidents of quantity, quality, action, and passion,[3] which is

---

[1] The case of Ockham's views, crucial in the development of semiotic consciousness for the challenge it posed already within the protosemiotic development (see Deely 2001: Chaps. 8 & 9), I examined more closely in Deely 2009a *passim* (= also in this case 2005a: 15–17 [summarized in Diagram 1 p. 16], 66–68, 71–72); and further in detail in Deely 2008b, esp. Chapter 5.

[2] Such as Thomas Aquinas, c.1254/6: *In I Sent.* d. 26 q. 2 art. 2c: "in relativis autem neutrum est sicut privatio alterius, vel defectum aliquem importans. cuius ratio est, quia in relativis non est oppositio secundum id quod relativum in aliquo est: sed secundum id quod ad aliud dicitur. unde quamvis una relatio habeat annexam negationem alterius relationis in eodem supposito, non tamen ista negatio importat aliquem defectum. quia defectus non est nisi secundum aliquid quod in aliquo natum est esse: unde cum id quod habet oppositionem relativam ad ipsum, secundum rationem oppositionis non ponat aliquid, sed ad aliquid, non sequitur imperfectio vel defectus; et ideo sola talis oppositio competit distinctioni personarum." — "Neither among related things is as the privation of the other, or as introducing some defect. The reason for this is that in relatives there is not an opposition according to that which is relative **in** something: but according to that which is said to be **toward** another. Whence even though one relation has connected with it the negation of another relation supposed in the same thing, yet this negation does not introduce any defect, because a defect obtains only in accordance with something which pertains to the proper constitution of a thing: whence, since that which has a relative opposition to that thing, according to the rationale of the opposition does not posit something, but rather *toward* something, an imperfection or defect does not follow upon the opposition as relative; and this is the reason why only an opposition of this sort and sense belongs to the distinction of persons" (in the Trinity).

[3] *Ibid.*, ad 2: "… minima distinctio realis quae possit esse … tali distinctioni competit ens minimum, scilicet relatio." — "… the minimal distinction possible in the order of mind-independent being … pertains to that form of *ens reale* which is the least mind-independent, namely, the being of relation.

true if we consider exclusively the order of *ens reale* as what obtains independently of the finite mind.

Dependent upon individuals (the "*fundamenta remota*" or "subjects" of the relations) through their characteristics (the "*fundamenta proxima*"), the *relations themselves* linking individuals according to a certain order precisely *consisted in* that order as *irreducible* to the subjectivity of the individuals ordered with all their inherent characteristics,[4] as an army on the march differs from that same army in the disarray of flight signaling defeat of the soldiers — that same group of individuals with their same inherent characteristics unchanged in both cases.

The relations among things sometimes obtain in the physical world itself, the order of *ens reale*, in its being independent of the action of any finite mind. Sometimes, I say. For other times the relations in question obtain precisely and only through the action of some finite mind, as when Napoleon, seeing his army begin to collapse in disarray, rallies the men according to a pattern of relations he envisions in mind *in contrast to* the relations actually obtaining at the moment he undertakes the rally. If successful, the very pattern of relations envisioned will be transferred from thought and imagination into the conduct of the soldiers, who will by that very transferal turn imminent defeat back into the prospect of victory. Prospectivity, we might almost say, consequent upon the *only indirect* dependence of relation upon substance as the groundroot of subjectivity,[5] is the singular (precisely by reason of this indirectness) effect — the "indirect effect" of relations upon and within the physical world.

8.1. The Uniqueness of Relation in the Behavior of Animals

Now what is remarkable about relations in the behavior of animals is the very thing that made it possible for so many so long

---

[4] See Poinsot 1632a: *Tractatus de Signis*, Second Preamble "On Relation", Article 2, 88ff.

[5] See in this chapter subsection 8.3., p. 64ff. below.

to deny their reality as irreducible constituents of *ens reale* — irreducible, that is, to the individuals and characteristics of individuals in which Ockham, for example, famously declared the whole of *ens reale* to consist.

What is remarkable about relations, in fact, is actually twofold. We will come to the second peculiarity shortly.[6] Let us note that first of all, and perhaps most remarkable, is their *permeability* to the otherwise distinct orders of what does and what does not exist independently of finite mind. One and the same relation, existing under changing circumstances, can be one time real (*ens reale*) and one time unreal (*ens rationis*), so subtly that the creature anchoring the relations in any given case may be quite unaware of the difference — as the lover who continues on his way to meet his beloved blithely unaware that his beloved had been crushed by a meteor only minutes earlier en route to the same rendezvous.

What I mean here by "permeability" calls for fuller explanation, to be sure, which will come in Chapter 9 below, particularly in Section 9.2. But here let me at least say this much, by way of anticipation. I am referring to the fact that relations are the *only* form of finite being that can continue to exist with positive essence or character unchanged when the circumstances under which they came into existence — whether from mind or from nature — *have* changed so drastically that the relation in question no longer pertains to its order of origin, even though it continues to exist. Student A goes to a final exam and provides a cover story, an alibi, for his room-mate, student B, who was too hung-over to wake up in time for the exam. The worried student A reports to the strict professor that student B got taken to the emergency room (to ensure that the professor will allow a make-up), then rushes through his own exam in order to get back in time to square his story with what his room-mate will say to the exam professor. Upon arriving back at the room, however, student A finds student B gone, and is panic-stricken with the fear that student B has gone to the

---

[6] See below, p. 63, and Chaper 9 following.

examination room and the professor has found out that student A lied to him.

Student A rushes next door and asks his neighbor in a panicked voice, "Where's Joey?" "Oh", the neighbor says, "he got up about ten minutes after you left and tried to rush to exam, but he tripped and cracked his head open. They had to take him to the emergency room." So the relation of student B to the emergency room, which started out as a lie, turned out to be true, simply by reason of circumstances beyond both the knowledge and the control of student A! Student A is visibly relieved by the neighbor's report — not because he is glad Joey cracked his skull, but because he no longer has to worry that he will be in trouble with the professor for having lied. That is an example of what I mean by the "permeability of relations to the otherwise distinct orders of what does and what does not exist independently of the mind".

The case involves several perplexities. Poinsot was, if not the first, certainly one of the first so to treat the matter as to make unmistakable that "relations of reason" are actually extremely poorly named. What most fundamentally contrasts the order of *ens reale* to the order of *ens rationis* so-called is not the fact that *reason*, species-specifically human understanding, forms the latter, but rather the fact that the order of *ens rationis* so-called has its proper existence from the cognitive activity of a finite mind and has no existence without that activity supervening, *regardless of whether the "mind" in question is rational or not.*

And the point goes deeper than this. The animal, *rational or not,* perforce constructs *a plethora* of *entia rationis* unwittingly, not as such, but as facilitating its function and orientation within the environment.[7] In short, the objective presence of *entia rationis* in the experience of cognitive organisms is not an optional but a neces-

---

[7] The semiotically sophisticated will recognize here the monumental contribution of Jakob von Uexküll with his "Umwelttheorie": see Kull ed. 2001; and, for the Thomistic context, Pieper 1952 and Deely 2004f. The problem of fully defining the Umwelt in semiotic terms I have addressed in Deely 2001b, and again in the Appendix to 2002: 126–143.

sary one in order for the bare physical surroundings to become a meaningful world, an Umwelt, as we will see, in which the organism has its central place. In other words, "beings of reason" are formed and function wherever there are in nature cognitive organisms that need to orient themselves within their surroundings in order to survive and thrive. Thus, "relations of reason", so-called, in fact are found wherever cognitive organisms are found *active as cognitive* within the physical universe.[8] They are not only objective relations; they are *purely* objective relations.

To call them "beings of reason", then, is not without its grounds,[9] for only understanding in its difference from perception (*phantasiari*[10]) is capable of discriminating between mind-dependent and mind-independent aspects as such within objectivity (for exactly the same reason that only understanding is capable of discriminating relations as such from things that are related in objectivity). But, more often, the so-calling amounts to a manifestation of an excess of the anthropomorphism according to which only beings *recognized* as mind-dependent (which requires a critical rational comparison) are to be *called* mind-dependent (and so receive their name as *entia rationis* from the faculty of reason which is presupposed to the critical comparison necessary to their recognition). This conceit, however, overlooks the fact that such beings exist normally before they are ever recognized for what they are.[11] Were

---

[8] This is a crucial point for the understanding of semiosis, yet it is a point seldom or never emphasized or even made at all in traditional presentations and discussions of objective being. See Poinsot's remarks in his 1632 *Tractatus de Signis*, First Preamble "On Mind-Dependent Being", Article 3, "By What Powers and through Which Acts Do Mind-Dependent Beings Come About?", 66/47–68/34, esp. 67/1–19 & 73/17–74/9.

[9] See Poinsot 1632: *Treatise on Signs*, loc. cit., 68/35–71/19, esp. 69/13–48, and 71/20– 72/17, 73/16–74/9, 75/1–21, 76/18–37. But this point will be taken up and clarified directly in Chap. 9 below, Section 9.3., esp. p. 76, text and note 2.

[10] On this important term, see notes 1–4 in Poinsot 1632: 240–242.

[11] Objectivity is precisely the existence of anything (real or unreal) *as known*. By contrast, subjectivity is the existence of anything as having an individual identity *separate* from other individuals and *independently* of being objectified or apprehended. Suprasubjectivity, or the being proper to relations, mind-dependent or

this not so, how much of human history would be different! The witches at Salem, to mention nothing of those in the European main lands of the 15th and 16th centuries, would hardly have been burned had the truth of their alleged witchcraft been perceived by the understanding of those who judged them.

Go back as far as you like, as far as you can into the increasing darkness of human history: there are the gods, countless rivals making their demands, including (not so infrequently) human sacrifices, if all is to be well in the particular world of some human group. The gods are always with us, though we do not always know who they are. No. Normally, "beings of reason" exist and operate in the orientative behavior of all animals, including human animals, long before they come to be recognized as such, and even if they are never recognized as such (which is always the case, in fact, among the animals other than human).

The cat stalking its prey knows well and has to know well, in order not to go hungry, if the prey is moving to the right or to the left. Yet the relations which allow the animal to orientate itself thus before pouncing have no reality apart from *the animal's* objective world, within which world the system of orientation is precisely a network of real *and* unreal relations making the subjectivities of the physical environment *objectivities* organized along quite other lines than those that pertain to their subjectivity alone.[12] These relations determine objectively the social reality — over and above *ens reale* — in which both predator and prey are living and moving and

---

mind-independent, is that *mode* of existence dependent upon subjectivity but contrasting to it as what *links* one thing to another contrasts with what *separates* one thing from another. This linkage may spring from psychological or from physical nature, or both; but only *reason* (i.e., human understanding) can recognize the difference between relation as such and the subjective fundament or ground of the relation, as also between relations provenating here from physical and there from psychological subjectivity. It is this last distinctiveness of reason that warrants the otherwise unwarrantable traditional designation of mind-dependent relations as "*entia rationis*". See the full discussion in Deely 2001: 350–354.

[12] See Cajetan 1507: Q. 1, Art. 3 (Rome: 2 May 1507); Poinsot 1632: *Treatise on Signs*, 149/46, 179n13; 187/35, 188n33; 270/38.

having their being (for as long as they have being). They are not "in the mind" of the cat: they precisely connect or relate what is "in the cat" *to* what is "outside the cat", namely, its prey.

8.1.1. Signs between animal and world

Any such network of relations by which an animal marks and stalks its prey, or finds its way home, is precisely a "semiotic web" (as Sebeok famously termed the phenomenon),[13] without which the animal could neither find its way and prey nor long survive as an organism.

A physical stimulus, a sound, let us say: what is it? Heard, "what it is" depends in part on the one hearing. Let us say the sound in question is the howl of a wolf. To another wolf, the howl may become a sign of lust, while to a sheep that same howl is a signal of danger. What the other wolf cathects positively, the sheep cathects negatively. And note carefully: in neither case is the "interpretation" a pure matter of subjectivity. The sound originates outside the other wolf and the sheep. The hearing of the howl occurs outside the sound itself, as does the interpretation or cathecting of the sound which takes place, respectively, inside the other wolf and inside the sheep.

8.1.2. Signs within animals

But even what takes place "inside" the two animals does not end there. On the contrary, what takes place inside the respective animals serves to relate them respectively, the one positively, the other negatively, to the source of the sound which is emphatically external to and independent of them both. Inside and outside are correlated, so far as the animal's orientation is involved. There is no "outside" without a correlated "inside" constituting objectivity, even though the subjectivities involved in objectivity exceed what is object *both* on the side of the cognizing and cathecting organism *and* on the side of the physical surroundings enabling that organism to survive (or imperiling it) here and now.

---

[13] Sebeok 1975.

Objectivity, we may go so far as to say, insofar as it involves sensation at least, is the partial internalization within my subjectivity of the subjectivities that surround me and exist independently of my awareness. This "partial internalization" is precisely what founds my relations to my surroundings. These relations, in turn, transform mere things into objects of my concern or disdain, and these objects transcend mere things to constitute an objective world in principle distinct from and irreducible (in its objectivity) to the world of things as physical and "given" at once prejacently to and concurrently with my awareness of *that* world of physical subjectivities and intersubjectivities as included partially within (though far from exhausting) my horizon of concerns, my Umwelt, my "objective world".

In other words, we confront here one of the irreducible characteristics of *relation* in its contrast to the subjectivity of all that separates a given individual organism from the rest of the environment, and of all that separates the various components of the environment from one another in *their* individual physical being. We confront here relation, if not in what is distinctive of it as relation simply, at least in what is distinctive of it as relation enters into and forms the fabric of the experience of animals, namely, the fact that relation *connects invisibly* two or more individuals through a common third. Or rather, I should say, we confront here, even within the relations constituting experience, the distinctive *permeability* whereby *it makes no difference* to the being and function of the relation as such whether its suprasubjective being provenates from mind or from nature first of all, or even from both simultaneously. And this feature of relations within experience stems directly from what is distinctive to the being of relations as such as elements partially constituting the order of *ens reale*, "hardcore reality", the order of subjective or physical individualities making up the environmental world in its being independent of cognitive activity[14] at any given time and place.

---

[14] Finite cognitive activity, not to put too fine a point on it.

8.1.3. Signs in the world

Take the howl of the wolf simply as a vibration in the air, a physically detectable phenomenon, recordable on a suitable instrument, measurable. Impinging on the hearing here of the other wolf, there of the sheep, it establishes a real relation of physical dependency of the hearing organs on something other than themselves, namely, the stimulus arising from the external source of the first wolf's vocal apparatus. This relation of physical dependency is a relation of cause and effect, as we might say, noting even here that the *relation* is over and above the cause *and* the effect *equally.*

The effect, in this case twofold (a stimulation and specification of, first, the hearing of this sheep, and, second, of that wolf), in turn becomes the basis for *a yet further relation,* not a physical one but a cognitive or interpretive one whereby the source of the howl to which the other wolf and the sheep are related by hearing, that same source is now in turn related to the other wolf and to the sheep, respectively, as "something to be sought" in the first case and "something to be avoided" in the second case. This relation — in the twofold case interpretive, no doubt — compared to the first one which was simply physical from stimulus to sense organ, is comparatively unreal, mind-dependent as compared to mind-independent; yet it serves no less in the enabling of the diverse animals to orientate themselves respecting their surrounding environment.

Note too that it is precisely the weaving together of these two relations, one comparatively real (i.e., obtaining in the order of *ens reale*), the other comparatively unreal (i.e., obtaining first of all in the order of *ens rationis,* and thence constituting a reality *socially constituted*), that comprises the stimulus as an *object of experience* and not just merely a recordable sound obtaining in the environment as a vibration whether any organism hears it or not.

So we find that what makes the difference between objects and things — where the former term designates anything cognized or known as such (anything apprehended in whatever way) while the latter term designates anything as existing whether or not any organism has an awareness of it — is again this peculiar being, this so-called *ens minimum,* of relation as obtaining (whenever and wherever and to whatever extent it obtains) *suprasubjectively,* obtaining *over and above* whatever subjects it unites or fails to unite.

8.2. The Phenomenon of Mistakes ("Fallibilism")

But consider the case of a mistaken interpretation. The 19th century, the last of the fully "modern" centuries, located a mistaken interpretation psychologically, "inside the head" of the one mistaken, a "state of its brain", as the analytic identity hypothesis would have it. Indeed, something presumably went on there in the organism's nervous system, but whatever it was cannot be understood wholly to absorb the mistake. For no relation as such can be reduced to the individual or subjective characteristics of the individual upon which the relation depends and from which the relation arises to whatever extent it serves to connect that individual with whatever it is that the individual is not but stands in relation *to.* "The mistake" in its psychological reality connected the one mistaken to something other than himself or herself, something "objective" *in just the way that anything is really objective*: by existing as apprehended, "mistakenly" or not, at the terminus of a relation.

Here we reach a point where it becomes necessary to explicitate the second aspect of the twofold peculiarity of relation introduced above as prelude to commenting on the singular permeability of relation to the otherwise opposed orders of *ens reale* and *ens rationis.* Not only is it peculiar to relation to be able to pass back and forth in its proper being between the physical and the objective orders (individuals in their subjectivity cannot do this, but are confined *as subjective* to the determinately real order — the order of *ens reale* — even when in their very subjectivity, as happens often enough, they are also objectified as the terminus of cognitive and cathectic relations). It is further peculiar to relations[15] to be the *only* mode of being that the finite mind can, by its properly cognitive activity,

---

[15] Aquinas c.1266: I, q. 28, art. 1; commentary in Poinsot 1632: Second Preamble "On Relation", esp. Art. 2, 93/16–98/40; but see also his First Preamble "On Mind-Dependent Being", Art. 3, 69/13–40.

form under any circumstances. The point is important enough to deserve treatment in a chapter of its own (Chapter 9 following).

But even at the risk of some repetition and anticipation at the same time, let us not leave the question of what is unique about relations without doing our very best (Section 8.3. following) to close the door upon what has proved to be, over philosophy's many centuries since Aristotle's attempts at delineating categories of *ens reale*, the single greatest obstacle to understanding the distinctive and (for the action or causality that follows upon the being proper to and constitutive of signs) most decisive feature of relation's uniqueness among the modes of mind-independent being, and that is the presentation of those categories with only the consideration of subjectivity placed front and center (with the distinction between substance as being in itself and accident as being in another), rather than the consideration of intersubjectivity as irreducible to subjectivity (with the distinction between being in and being toward).

To speak of the uniqueness of relation in this case is not enough, for *every* mode of mind-independent being that belongs to a distinct *category* thereof, after all, is "unique" — otherwise it would not belong to a distinct category; and this is true of substance no less than accidents, and of inherent accidents modifying the subjectivity of substance no less than of the intersubjectivity distinguishing relations as actually tying together substances as a consequence not only of formal properties but also of interactions (while yet distinct therefrom as *continuing* to be, like an offspring resulting from sexual interaction, as long as circumstances permit long after the interactions, if not the subjects that interacted, have ceased to occur).

8.3. A Singularity Beyond the Uniqueness of Relation as a Mode of Ens Reale

According to Aristotle's main intention in formulating his tentative lists of categories — which was not first of all for considerations of logic as the instrument of thought (as is often argued) but first of all for considerations of physics in being able to specify the ways in which an existence independent of finite mind can be verified — relation proved, then and now, the most troublesome, the most elusive to establish as irreducible respecting the other elements constitutive of τo ὀν, *ens reale*, being insofar as it exists independently of the wishes, desires, awareness, or beliefs of any finite mind.

For Aristotle himself, it took no less than three tries[16] — a case of "three strikes and you're in" — before he succeeded to identify an *esse ad* which did not reduce to some instance of *esse in*: but succeed he did, and was so relieved to have done so that he returned without further ado to refocus on his original point, which had been to distinguish substance from every form of accident. As a result, it does not seem so much as to have occurred to him to refocus the discussion so as to place front and center the requirement for philosophical thought concerning the world of nature to see that the division of *ens reale* as material being into substance and (or vis-à-vis) accidents as modifications of but dependent upon substantial being is a starting point that all but hides from view and virtually guarantees the overlooking of the point about relation which distinguishes it not merely *within* the order of ens reale as one among the other types of accidents, but further *in contrast to whole order of* τo ὀν *in its "reale" character:* in contrast to not merely the "other accidents" taken as unique modes of being and to substance as the unique basic mode upon which all accidents depend, but in contrast also to substance *along with* all *other* of its accidental modes taken together as comprising the complete order of *ens reale*, yet far from the complete order of being as objective. For this, even *intersubjectivity*, indeed the feature of *ens reale* distinctive of and unique to relation among the categories, in *not enough*.

Yet even the sight of this irreducible uniqueness of relation remained effectively blocked to the majority of Aristotle's followers and commentators in the succeeding centuries. Grote (1872), to take perhaps the outstanding English example, astonishingly fails to see that the category of relation in Aristotle does not merely mean that substances have to be understood in causal connection and in-

---

[16] See "The fundamental architecture of the Treatise on Signs" in Deely 1985: EA 472–479, esp. notes 112, 113, 114, where the original Greek of Aristotle's wrestling with the point is cited.

teraction with things other than themselves (that there is a *relativum secundum dici* in the terms of Aquinas and Poinsot), but further and more basically means that subjectivity is not enough to constitute the whole of the reality of finite being as mind-independent.[17]

8.3.1. *A new first step toward understanding hardcore reality*

So perhaps today, in order to get the point of postmodernity as a new epoch in philosophy's history as a whole, the single most important first step Aristotelians or anyone else talking about "reality" has to take is to abandon the approach to the question of hardcore reality which begins by distinguishing between individuals and their characteristics, substance and accidents. For history in every previous age — ancient Greek philosophy, the Latin interval, modern times — amply demonstrates that most thinkers who have taken this starting point never reach an understanding of the positive uniqueness of relation, let alone its further singularity.

The first step should not be one that hides or buries relation in the order of subjectivity upon which relation depends, along with substance and its direct modifications (which is what all other accidents amount to and reduce to). The history of discussion on these questions amply demonstrates that the first step ought to be one that puts what is *different* about relation in contrast with *all* other accidents, and not merely with substance, rather than one which emphasizes instead what all accidents including relation have in common, namely, a dependence upon substance in order to be; for even in the matter of this shared characteristic of dependency it is important to note what is not noted in the traditional discus-

---

[17] Says Grote (I quote from the 2nd ed. of 1880, pp. 80–81, having misplaced my own copy of the 1872 1st ed.) of Aristotle: "he both conceives and defines the Category of Relation or Relativity (*Ad Aliquid*) in a way much narrower than really belongs to it. If he had assigned to this Category its full and true comprehension, he would have found it implicated with all the other nine. None of them can be isolated from it in predication." *Compare Poinsot 1632: Second Preamble "On Relation", Article 2, 81/1–11 & 89/24–90/12*: in Poinsot's terms, Grote, in mistaking transcendental relation for the whole import of relative being, in effect seconds Ockham's brushing aside of ontological relation itself as anything more than an *ens rationis*.

sions — to wit, while all other accidents depend directly upon the being of substance, relation as such depends only indirectly *through* the other accidents. This is the reason why Aquinas terms relation *ens minimum* in the order of *ens reale*, but, as we will see, it is also the reason why relation turns out to be *ens maximum et solum* in the order of *ens rationis* in particular and *ens obiectivum* in general though not *solum* (even as it proves to be, in theology, the reason why the unity of the Godhead is not compromised by the Trinity of Persons, in the explanation of Aquinas[18]).

8.3.2. What sets relation apart from the whole of subjectivity, not only apart from substance as an "accident"

What distinguishes relation not only from substance but also from every other accidental instance of being is that it does not itself positively instantiate subjectivity. Substance does instantiate subjectivity, as do also the inherent characteristics or modifications of substance — in other words, all accidents *except* relation as such (or relation as involved with other accidents, as I succeeded to demonstrate in the discussion surrounding the *Four Ages* diagram of Aristotle's most complete list of the categories[19]) belong to the order within *ens reale* of *being in, inesse* — being in another in the case of accidents, being in itself in the case of substance. By contrast, relation, though it depends upon subjective modifications of substance in order to obtain, does not in any case reduce to those subjective modifications and is not itself one of them. Which is but to say that subjectivity does not include relations directly but only indirectly, through the subjective modifications upon which the relation depends for providing it with a fundament — a fundament without which the relation would not obtain as an intersubjective *ens reale*.

---

[18] See Aquinas 1266: *Summa theologiae*, First Part, Question 28, "Whether there are real relations in God?", along with the discussion and analysis in Poinsot 1632: "Second Preamble On Relation", Article 2 "On what is required for a relation in the order of mind-independent being", esp. the "Resolution of Counter-Arguments" *Primo*, 93/17–96/36.

[19] Deely 2001: 73–78, summary diagram on p. 77.

8.3.3. *Taking the new first step: foregrounding instead of backgrounding the being of relation*

So the first step toward understanding reality in its hardcore aspect as well as Aristotle's categories thereof would best be to distinguish, not substance from accidents, but relation from substance *and* accidents alike as *inter*subjectivity in contrast to *subjectivity* in whatever form. Thus the first step had best be one which *foregrounds*, not backgrounds, the being of relation among and within Aristotle's categories, as intersubjectivity contrasts with subjectivity. Being in itself distinguished from being in another, substance contrasted with accident, alone doesn't cut it. This traditional approach or initial stance, so entrenched as to border on standing as an immovable obstacle to the understanding of relation (and hence semiosis as the action and indirect, prospective causality consequent upon the being proper to signs), *backgrounds* — not to say *buries* — the key feature for even beginning to start to commence to realize the being proper to relation as that being alone makes semiosis in nature possible in the first place, wherever signs are at work in nature, actually or only virtually, as circumstances determine.

So let us make as our first step to distinguish *being in* from *being toward*, *inesse* from *adesse*, not substance from accident, individual from its distinguishing characteristics. Then, once we are clear about, or at least enroute to becoming clear about, the contrast and difference between subjectivity and intersubjectivity we can introduce the distinction *within* subjectivity between substance as being in itself (or subjectivity in its root and ground), and those accidents which are direct modifications of the subjectivity of substance and hence themselves as well as (or through) substance direct positive instances of subjectivity.

8.3.4. *Dependency in being is not univocal because it is not direct only*

Since accidents all depend upon substance in order to be, and intersubjective accidents depend upon subjective accidents in order to be, we see at once that relation is unique not only in its transcending of subjectivity as a whole but also in depending upon the subjectivity of substance only indirectly, while all other accidents depend directly upon the subjectivity of substance. So we have a hierarchy: relation as an accident depends upon the inherent accidents (direct modifications of substance) in order to be, and so *indirectly* upon substance itself, while in order to be the inherent accidents depend *directly* upon substance.

8.3.5. Prescissing the singularity beyond relation's mind-independent uniqueness

Good. With this much clear we are at last in a position to behold what is not only unique but at the same time *singular* about the being proper to relation: in order to be intersubjective, relation as a mode of being must *first* (logically, now, not necessarily temporally) and *simultaneously* be *suprasubjective*. And while intersubjectivity is perforce and necessarily *also* suprasubjective, suprasubjectivity is not at all also and necessarily intersubjective.

Here we come up against the medieval Latin insight borrowed by Brentano (if, unfortunately, also radically distorted in the taking[20]) from the Latin Age philosophers: what distinguishes mental events (or, as we might say, psychological states, adding cathectic as well as cognitive) from the subjectivity of material realities is that the former necessarily while the latter only contingently (depending upon circumstance) are "of" or "about" something other than themselves.

What this means is that psychological states serve always to provenate or provide the fundament or ground of a relation as suprasubjective, whether or not that relation is *also* (again depending upon circumstances) intersubjective or not.

There is the singularity of relation: as suprasubjective in essence it not only *transcends* the subjective order *tout court*, it is also *in its*

---

[20] Brentano 1874; contrast with Deely 2007, and see the analysis in Deely 1978, esp. as subtitled "The idealist root of Husserl's phenomenology" and reprinted in Cobley Ed. 2009: 252–265.

positive being **indifferent** to that order. Truly and really to be a relation it does not have to be in the category of relation as an instance of mind-independent being.

And so we find on the side of "being toward" contrasted with "being in" — *and only on the side of being toward* — the further distinction between being which is and being which is not independent of being apprehended by a finite mind, the very root or ground from which springs the difference between (a) objective being which may or may not be also subjective and (b) subjective being which may or may not *happen* to be apprehended but which, along with whatever intersubjectivities it may sustain, cannot positively be at all except insofar as it has some independence of being apprehended within a finite awareness.

8.3.6. How the singularity of relation makes unlimited semiosis possible

Now human beings are semiotic animals precisely because they are the only animals capable so of using signs as to be aware that they are signs, which means to recognize that the material objects we perceive as signs are such not by reason of their subjective constitution but only by reason of their involvement in a triadic relation as standing in the foreground position of representing something other than themselves, something that they themselves are not. The semiosic animal (there is no other kind!) need not perceive but the semiotic animal must needs be able to grasp by understanding the difference between related subjectivities and the *relations themselves* as realities over and above those perceived subjectivities related — even though directly imperceptible as such! By reason of such an (intellectual) awareness directly of the imperceptible being of relations, then, the semiotic animal can in turn take these *relations themselves* and not merely the perceptibly related things as "models" or "foundations" for the formation in the Innenwelt of yet other relations: as it were, for "relations founded upon relations", something impossible in the order of *ens reale* in its contrast with *ens rationis*, in the order of physical being as contrasted with objective being even as including something of physical being — something that cannot occur in the order of subjectivities and intersubjectivities as mind-independent,[21] but only within the order of mind-dependent being itself as suprasubjective necessarily while intersubjective only contingently.[22] (This is the origin of what Sebeok so presciently termed "language in the root sense", the ability cognitively to manipulate relations in their difference from related things, an ability which, through exaptation, becomes the species-specific reality of linguistic communication among semiotic animals.)

8.3.7. The view from the new standpoint

In the order of *ens reale* relations are necessarily intersubjective, that is, tied to some contingent subjectivity or other *both* as their fundament *and* as their terminus. But in the order of objectivity, relations are only contingently intersubjective, while remaining in both orders necessarily (indeed, in order to *be* relations at all) suprasubjective. Hence the parent of a dead child must cease indeed to be a parent in the order of *ens reale*,[23] but there is also the dimension within objectivity of mind-dependent being, and here the relation expunged as an intersubjectivity continues in full force to obtain suprasubjectively! October 7, 1501, may have no foothold in the thought of most Americans, for example, but the battle of Lepanto from that date still lived in the mind of Osama bin Laden as a festering wound, a motive of attack and cause for revenge!

A substance is not a substance unless it be in the category of substance. An accident directly modifying substance cannot occur

---

[21] See Poinsot 1632: Second Preamble, Article 3, 102/24–25, the *prima difficultas*, "an ipsaemet relationes reales possint fundare alias" ("whether one mind-independent relation can be the foundation of yet another such relation"), discussed at 102/35–105/13. Further in Chap. 9, p. 76n2.

[22] Ibid., First Preamble, Article 2, 61/40–62/16, esp. 62/7–12; but *note well*, from Article 3, 71/21–72/16 (esp. 72/11–16) and 76/19–32, that "reflexivity" in the sense available only to semiotic animals remains *always secondary* in the formation of mind-dependent being as part of an Umwelt.

[23] See the discussion around this point (When a child dies, in what sense is the child's parent a parent?) in Deely 1990: Chapter 4.

unless it be in the category of accident. But a relation need not be in the accidental category of relation in order to be a relation. For the categories — as Aristotle conceived them — are divisions of *ens reale*, while relations need not fall in a category of *ens reale* in order to be relations.[24] That is why, as Poinsot pointed out in the opening paragraphs of his *Tractatus*, the being of relations is what enables the action of signs as transcending the difference between purely objective being and objective being which is also partially subjective or intersubjective, because relations, and relations alone, in their positive essence or being transcend the divide within being as mind-dependent or mind-independent, with whatever subdivisions thereof one may care to enumerate or mention.

So must we say of relation that it is not only unique within the order of *ens reale*, but singular in constituting the only form of being that transcends the opposition of *ens reale* to *ens rationis*. Relation thus is the ground of objectivity and semiosis alike in their proper possibility, but objects become objects fully and actually only through the virtuality of semiosis as underlying all that is or can become objective, as we may now turn to see.

---

[24] Poinsot 1632: 95/18–40: "Quomodo autem hoc sit peculiare in relatione et in aliis generibus non inveniatur, dicimus ex eo esse, quia in aliis generibus ratio propria et formalissima eorum non potest positive intelligi, nisi entitative etiam intelligatur, quia positiva eorum ratio est ad se tantum et absoluta, et ideo non intelligitur positive nisi etiam entitative, quod enim est ad se, entitas est. Sola relatio habet esse ens et ad ens, et pro ea parte, qua se habet ad ens, positive se habet, nec tamen inde habet entitatem realem." — "But how this is peculiar to the case of relation and is not found in the other categories, we say is owing to the fact that in the other categories their proper and most formal rationale cannot be understood positively unless it is also understood entitatively, because their positive rationale is toward themselves only and subjective, and for this reason is not understood positively unless also entitatively; for that which is toward itself is an entity. Only relation has [both] to be being and toward being, and from that content by which it is toward being, it exists positively, yet it does not have thence the rationale of being mind-independent."

Chapter 9

The Being of All Objects as Objects Derives From but Only Sometimes Reduces To the Being of Relations

This conclusion, that relations are the *only* mode of being that the finite mind can form by its properly cognitive activity, may appear to be too strong, and the surprising element of the claim does not help. The idea, however, is not originally mine but something I became persuaded of from reading Aquinas and some of his commentators, Poinsot in particular, as I have indicated in the notes of the section just concluded, but also Maritain. What Aquinas pointed out was that *ens reale* always and inevitably has a certain priority in the life of animals, both because the external senses make no use of mental representations ("*species expressae*" in protosemiotic terms, "ideas or images" in modern parlance) in their prescissively distinctive proper activity, and because if *ens reale* were not attained in the perceptions of animals there would long since have ceased to be animals.

9.1. The Priority in Experience of Being Which Is Not Purely Objective

What Aquinas said was that, when the mind makes up objects of its own devising — fictions, as it were — it can do so only on the pattern of the experience of beings which are not dependent on experience in order to be. Now beings which are not dependent on experience in order to be, according to Aquinas, as earlier to Aristotle, reduce ultimately to substances with their inherent accidents (individuals with their subjective characteristics, let us say) *along with* those relations among substances without which the substances either would not have come into being in the first place or would not continue in being here and now.

Yet take careful note of this: even these beings not dependent upon experience in order to be are dependent upon experience in order to *become known*: for anything to be known, regardless of any further being it may or may not have or acquire, the being in question must have a relation to the one aware of it, and it is this relation that may be said, in that sense, to constitute, but not to determine, the awareness. What *determines* the awareness as of this, say, rather than that, is not so much the relation as suprasubjective but the relation as terminating here rather than there. Thus the *terminus* of the relation provides the object determining the awareness, but the relation itself as founded or grounded in the animal become aware constitutes the awareness here and now. Given Aquinas's point that animals depend on the experience of things objectified as not of their own devising in order further to devise their own objects,[1] we can say that the patterns given in experience according to which the cognitive organism may form mind-dependent objects or as-

---

[1] This is exactly the point of the prescissive distinction Aquinas makes between *sentire* as exclusively involving *species impressae* and *phantasiari* as involving also *species expressae*. In modern English we have "sensation" as counterpart to *sentire*, but the terms *species impressae* and *expressae* are without equivalents in modern philosophy (Maritain 1959: 115; Deely 2007: Chapter 4 and *passim*). This is also true, though to a considerably lesser extent, of the term *phantasiari*. For insofar as this term contains the notion of objects perceived in awareness *whether or not present here and now* in physical existence, it finds only a limited counterpart in the modern term "perception", which tends to be limited to the interpretation of things as objects physically at hand within our awareness.

For an attempt to establish (or re-establish) for the postmodern context the notion of the *species*, both 'impressed' and 'expressed', as "specifying form", see the extended discussions in *Intentionality and Semiotics* (Deely 2007); and for the full notion of perception as *phantasiari* in Aquinas, specifically, see the 1985 edition of Poinsot 1632: notes 1–4 on pp. 240–241, and Deely 1971, now incorporated as Reading 4 in Cobley Ed. 2009.

pects of objects are either intersubjective modes of being (real relations) or subjective modes of being (substances with their inherent
accidents) — in sum, things as interacting and interrelated.

9.2. The Two Modes of Purely Objective Being

Now when the cognitive organism forms a fictional entity on
the pattern of an intersubjective mode of being — a mode of being
actually connecting two or more real individuals — the resulting
object *is* interobjectively exactly what its model *also is* intersubjec-
tively, namely, a relation. Whence such a mind-dependent being is
properly called a "relation", albeit a mind-dependent one. It is not,
as mind-dependent, what its pattern is, namely, mind-independent;
but it is, as a relation, a suprasubjective mode of union, exactly what
its pattern *also* is.

But when the cognitive organism forms a fictional entity —
such as a vampire, or blindness — on the pattern of a subjective
mode of being, the resulting object *is not* what its model *is*, for its
model is *both* objectively *and also* subjectively existing, whereas the
fictional entity is existing *only* objectively. In the subjective order it
is *an absence*.

Consider the second case in detail: neither is this fictive or
constructed object, as mind-dependent, what its pattern is, namely,
mind-independent; nor is it, as something 'patterned after', what
its pattern is, namely something existing subjectively and hence in
the order of *ens reale* as well as *ens objectivum*. Just the opposite! As
existing objectively, what is known exists *relative to* its subjective
pattern or ground, whereas the pattern exists relative to *itself*. Such
"beings", Aquinas says, are, accordingly, well-termed *negations*, for,
positively considered, they *are* relations, hence they *are not* what
their pattern *is*: hence they are "negations" — the negatives of that
which they positively represent.

The model *after which* negations are formed is an *ens reale*. But
their being, their own being as "negations", is a being-modeled —
that is to say, a "being patterned after" (that is to say: a relation
positively speaking). Precisely this consequence is what needs to be

drawn out: that, accordingly, "negations" as objective are themselves mind-dependent relations,[2] no less than are the mind-dependent relations directly patterned after mind-independent relations, and for one and the same reason, to wit, that relation is the only form of being capable as such of existing objectively outside the order of *ens reale*, of finite being as mind-independent.[3]

Whence the conclusion, both surprising and ineluctable: if fictional beings, negations (imitations of subjectivity) no less than fictional relations (imitating physical relations), are unexceptionally in their proper being reducible positively to relations as

---

[2] Strictly (see note following), *termini* of mind-dependent relations; but every relation, dependent upon or independent of mind, is what constitutes *both* fundament *as* fundament (in contrast to those cases where a fundament is a subjective characteristic that would continue as an individuating feature though no longer as fundament were the relation it futher founds in the mind-independent order to cease existing) *and* the terminus *as* terminus, as I have several times had occasion analytically to presciss — e.g., 2007: 125–130; 2008b: 32n4, 44, 47–49, 64, 69; 2009a: 36–37, 62n5; etc.

[3] Poinsot 1632: "First Preamble" On Mind-Dependent Being, 53/37–45: "Sola vero relatio, quia non dicit solum conceptum 'in', sed etiam conceptum 'ad', ratione cuius praecise non dicit existentiam in se, sed extrinsecam termini attingentiam, ideo non repugnat concipi sine realitate, atque adeo ut ens rationis, concipiendo illud non ut in alio vel ut in se, sed ut ad aliud cum negatione existentiae in aliquo." — "Relation alone among the ways being is capable of existing independently of finite awareness, because it bespeaks not only the concept of 'being in', but also the concept of 'being toward' (by reason of which latter notion precisely relation does not bespeak an existence in itself but the extrinsic attainment of a terminus), for which very reason relation can be conceived apart from a mind-independent status, and therefore also as a mind-dependent being, by conceiving that being neither as in another nor as in itself, but simply as toward another with the negation of an existence in another."

The 'negation', therefore, would be simply the terminus of such a relation as object, while the relation itself in turn could be objectified — taken as a model or "pattern after which" for yet another objectification without *inesse* — *ad infinitum* (which is precisely the ground of unlimited semiosis). See further, then, the "Second Preamble" On Relation, 102/35–105/13, esp. 103/15–17, on why relations in the order of *ens reale* can only be founded on subjective features of being, in contrast to relations in the order of *ens rationis* which can be patterned after suprasubjectivities regardless of their status as intersubjectivities ("First Preamble", esp. 61/33–62/16, etc.), following up on Chap. 8 p. 71 notes 21 & 22 above.

suprasubjective, then *whatever exists purely objectively reduces as such to a network of relations,* while whatever exists subjectively as well *includes* relations necessarily but *does not reduce to* those relations as to a network external to itself. The conclusion can also be represented diagrammatically:

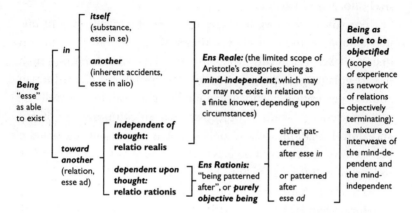

Diagram. *How Esse Objectivum Exceeds Ens Reale, or Why Categorial Being Is Inadequate to the Scope of Being as Experienced*

9.3. There Is a Rationale Common to Objects as Objects[4] Whether a Given Objectivity Be also Mind-Independent or Purely Objective

The key thing to understand is that the priority of *ens reale* over *ens rationis* emphasized by Aquinas is more an ontological priority

---

[4] This theme runs throughout Poinsot's systematization of the being proper to signs in bringing to its culmination the protosemiotic development launched by Augustine's initial descriptive definition of sign in general. It is fundamental to the point which Poinsot establishes but only implicitly for the doctrine of signs, to wit, the fact that the action of signs is prior to the being of objects as objects, and that the being of things is reached analytically only from within objectivity as an interweaving of *entia rationis* with the *entia realia* of the physical environment, as St. Thomas demonstrated in his showing that the "being" awareness of which formally differentiates understanding from sense-perception (*ens primum cognitum,* as he termed it) has for its first division within experience precisely the opposition of *ens rationis* as aspects of objectivity given in experience which reduce to the experience in which they are given (e.g., to give an example within anthroposemiosis, flag as sign of country) and *ens reale* as aspects of objectivity given in

than an experiential one, when the question concerns perceptual or intellectual experience ("ordinary experience" of the sort upon which cœnoscopy principally depends precisely in its contrast to the ideoscopy essential for developing science in the modern sense), and in contrast to the intellectual abstraction of a prescissively isolated sensation.

For when we move to the levels *either* of perception *or* of understanding — prescissively taken as such in contrast to sensation likewise taken (especially when we consider that sensation as such occurs normally, if not *always*, *within* perception, just as, for human animals, perception occurs *within* intellectual awareness as well) — we experience a world of objectivity woven compositively of real and unreal relations, whose only point is to present and sustain before us ready-to-hand objects of experience as to be sought (+), to be shunned (–), or safely to be ignored (0).

The fact that some among these objects before us are also present-at-hand, as things in their own right indifferent to any relation to us in objectivity, is *a later awakening, unique to the human animal*, as we will further discuss, and the source of the experience which leads the human animal to recognize that there is a difference between being and non-being, where being means precisely *ens reale* and non-being means precisely *ens rationis*. Being as first known by the human mind, *objective being*, transcends this distinction, and so cannot be identified with either term of the distinction (the *differentiation* of being which experience imposes over its course), even though *ens reale* maintains its ontological priority in the experiential discovery (through the subjective dimensions of the physical surroundings pressing their rights, as it were, in making the human animal recognize, unlike the other animals without language) that there is more to the being of the

---

experience which do not reduce to the experience in which they are given (e.g., clouds as signs of rain). See Deely 2001: Chap. 7, esp. 341–357; Deely 2002; and, as regards Poinsot's *Tractatus*, I refer the reader to the entries for OBJECT, OBJECTIVE PRESENCE, and OBJECTIVE UNION in the *Index Rerum* of the 1985 critical edition of Poinsot 1632: 552 column 1 – 554 column 1.

objective world than can be reduced to our experience of it or interests in it.

Only in this realization does the human animal become human, and only as human does the animal attain to the level of the possibility of metasemiosis, that is to say, of semiotics as the doctrine of signs. That is why, as Martinelli says,[5] "'animals' are not a category alien to human beings but are rather the category to which human beings belong"; and within this category the development of rationality is precursor to the discovery of semiosis.

Just as Aristotle's ζῷον λογον ἐχῶν was precursor to Porphyry's *animal rationale*, so the 'rational animal' was precursor to the semiotic animal, defining in terms of the subjectivity proper to human being what "semiotic animal" defines in terms of the objectivity distinctively attained by human animals[6] wherein it becomes possible not merely to distinguish things within objectivity but further to explore them as they are in themselves and to make the adjustments necessary from the metasemiosic standpoint for the well being of human life *precisely in its dependency* upon the semioses which link human animals within the signosphere with the forms

---

[5] Martinelli 2002: 2. See the pioneering work of Hoffmeyer 1993, 1996, and 2008 on the general notion of "biosemiotics". Also Deely 1991 and 2009e; Hoffmeyer and Emmeche 1999; Kull ed. 2001; Sebeok 2001a.

[6] Petrilli 1998: 8 (my translation): "In the full range of living things, and therefore of semiosis in general, human semiosis can be characterized as *metasemiosis* [see the discussion above, p. 32, note 10], that is to say, as the possibility of reflecting on the sign itself, of making the sign not only the object of an interpretation indistinguishable from a response to being, but more broadly of an interpretation with a reflection upon what the being is, with a suspension of response and with the possibility of deliberation. We could call this capacity for metasemiosis 'semiotics'. Giving a greater precision to Aristotle's just observation at the beginning of his *Metaphysics*, where he says that 'the human being tends by nature to knowledge', we could say that 'the human being tends by nature toward semiotics'. Human semiosis, anthroposemiosis, is distinguished by its capacity to appear as *semiotics*. Even if in the larger world of animals we can discern a prefiguration of 'reflection', of 'choice' and therefore of a momentary 'suspension of action' in function of a kind of 'metasemiosis', it is only in the human world that this metasemiosis realizes itself fully and literally in the sense that can be spoken of without any need of qualification. [It is] the distinction between semiosis interpretation and semiotic interpretation ...".

of life and semiosis by which the biosphere as a whole and the physical environment form "one system",[7] one "sphere of semiosis".

---

[7] Petrilli 1998: 181–182 (Petrilli's trans.): "relation with the infinite is not only a relation of the cognitive order but also a relation of involvement and responsibility — beyond the established order, beyond the symbolic order, beyond convention and habit — with what is most refractory to the totality, that is, the otherness of others, of the other person not as another self like ourselves, another alter ego, another member of the same community, but *other* in the sense of extraneousness, diversity, difference with respect to which indifference is not possible in spite of efforts and guarantees offered by identity of self.

"This aspect orients semiotics, investing it with a program which belongs to neither this nor that other ideology but which concerns the *prise de conscience* and consequent behavioral responsibility of the human being as a 'semiotic animal' for semiosis over the entire planet. For this reason global semiotics adequately founded on cognitive semiotics must open to a third sense characterizing these two 'semiotics' — beyond the quantitative and the theoretical — a third sense which is of the ethical order and may be characterized as 'teleosemiotics' (now 'semioethics').

"This trichotomy in semiotics seems important to us, even decisive, for the fulfillment of its commitment to the 'health of semiosis' and for its capacity to understand the entire semiosical universe which, obviously, is not separate from the capacity for listening and critique: 1) cognitive semiotics; 2) global semiotics; 3) teleosemiotics (now [Petrilli and Ponzio 2003, 2009; Deely 2004a; Deely, Petrilli, and Ponzio 2005]) *semioethics.*" See note 28 in the "Sequel" below, p. 123.

Chapter 10

Where Modern Philosophy Went Wrong: The Quasi-Fallacy of the External World

The human mind awakens to the objectivity of being only by being forced to recognize the subjectivities within objectivity opposed to the subjectivity of the mind itself. The "external world" is not discovered as external, it is discovered as a dimension within objects irreducible to our experience of them.[1]

The "problem of the external world" such as we find it in Descartes, Locke, and the moderns after them, not only Leibniz, Berkeley, and Hume, but including Kant, is not really a "critical problem" so much as it is a quasi-fallacy rooted in the failure to recognize the being proper and peculiar to relations with respect to the role they play in enabling awareness to exist at all,[2] particularly respecting the possibility of enabling there to be (for the semiotic animal at least) that correspondence between thought and being into the prior possibility of which Heidegger enquired as "the essence of truth".[3]

---

[1] See Deely 1994a and 2008b; Guagliardo 1993.

[2] It is the essence of nominalism, as it turns out, as Peirce was first to point out clearly. See Deely 2001: esp. Chaps. 8–10, and 15; now most completely in Deely 2008b.

[3] Heidegger 1943.

10.1. From Physical Environment to Objective World

Let us trace the levels.

In sensation, the physical environment impresses upon and specifies the organs of external sense to objectify aspects of the surroundings according to a pattern of relations which is naturally determined within the species (the biological type) of the organism doing the sensing. The differentiations of light that we call color, for example, reveal simultaneously in our awareness of them also shapes, positions, and movements; and so on for the other so-called "external" senses. Seeing a shape is logically posterior to and dependent upon seeing a color; but experientially and temporally the two are normally simultaneous. The relation of the logically prior to the posterior in this case is already a sign relation,[4] but a naturally determined one: given the nature of the organism sensing and the physical reality of the surroundings acting upon the organism's sense powers, what appears is the result of the two coming into relation.

In perception ("phantasiari", as the Latins put it),[5] by contrast, these same objectified aspects of the surroundings are interpreted and construed objectively on the basis of the needs and desires of the organism experiencing and elaborating the sensations. The result of the combination of sensory selection and perceptual interpretation is, in semiotics, famously termed an "Umwelt" after the researches of von Uexküll and glosses of Sebeok,[6] later translated precisely as "objective world" in the sense that phrase acquires in light of the realization of the difference in principle between objects and things.

An Umwelt, or objective world, thus, differs in principle from the physical environment, even though the objective world as objective necessarily includes aspects of the physical surroundings of

----

[4] See Poinsot 1632a: Book I, Question 6, esp. 206/38–207/7.

[5] See the extended footnote 2 on p. 240 of the 1985 critical edition of Poinsot 1632.

[6] See Kull ed. 2001; also Hoffmeyer and Emmeche eds. 1999, Deely 2005.

which we have become aware as elements of the meaningful world
within which the physical environment *also* but *not wholly* exists,
the objective world or Umwelt within which the organism sustains
and organizes its experiences of life. And how the Umwelt differs in
fact from the physical environment as such lies precisely in the fact
that, while the physical environment as such includes only mind-
independent relations, the objective world not merely includes but
is constituted in its public being by a *mixture* of mind-dependent
and mind-independent relations, a web woven indifferently (but
according to the biological constitution and heritage of the organism experiencing) of relations from the two orders.

Thus one and the same relation may be both objective and
physical at the same time; or a relation may be physical without
being also objective (i.e., without being known); or a relation may
be objective without also being physical. Think of the case (more
common than we are comfortable with) of a child who mistakenly identifies its father: the objective relation, thought to be real,
is in fact purely objective. Even though it is socially real, it is not
biologically real. But objects, although as objects they always obtain as termini of cognitive and cathectic relations, sometimes they
further obtain subjectively as well, to wit, when the objects known
are also things.

Insofar as the objects are things, they exist whether or not they
are known; but insofar as they are objects, they exist in a relation to
a knower, whether or not they are also things. Objects and things
vary relatively independently of one another, with the ontological
priority of *ens reale* over *ens rationis* nonetheless maintained thanks
to the unique character of sensation in its contrast to perception
and intellection alike in having no direct involvement of or dependence upon mental images ("species expressae" in the terminology
of Aquinas).[7] Both objects and things necessarily involve relations,
but things become objects *only* through the involvement of cognitive and cathectic relations, without which relations the objects as

---

[7] See Deely 2001: Chap. 7, esp. 345ff.; and Deely 2007 throughout.

objects disappear into virtuality, while the things objectified may remain as things (through the involvement of yet other unobjectified relations).

10.2. The World of Reality as Objective

Whatever may be the case in the order of *ens reale* on its own terms, where subjectivity is the strongest mode of being (even though necessarily involving also intersubjective relations without which even the subjectivity of the actual individual could neither come about nor continue over time), the order of objectivity has no subjectivity of its own but only relativizes physical subjectivity as the terminus of cognitive and cathectic relations wherein (and whereby) that subjectivity is subsumed into the objectivity of the suprasubjective network of relations constituting the experience and public world of any given organism, human or not. "In itself" the objective world consists wholly of the suprasubjective being proper to relations in their difference alike from the foundations whence they provenate and the termini on which they rest cognitively and cathectically. Objects appear as such only within this network, at the termini or reticles of the net, as it were, prey caught in the semiotic web. Fictional objects are part of that net, necessary to orient the organism even respecting the physical objects (or physical aspects of objects) that have as part of their being a subjectivity which establishes them in the order of *ens reale* as well as objectively.

The following three points need to be understood.

First, that objects fully actual differ in principle from things by reason of necessarily having what any given thing has only contingently, namely, a relation to a cognizing organism.

Second, this relation transforming thing into object is not a singular or isolated relation, but part of an entire network and field of relations comprising in fact nothing less than the experience itself of the organism wherein and whereby objects are given as this or that in the first place. As a consequence, even when it is a thing that is objectified, the objective being never simply reduces to, as if a mere reduplication of, the being of the thing as thing, but even the very thing objectified, as objectified, is inserted into a larger net of objectifying relations which present the thing as pertaining first of all to the needs and interests of the organism, not merely to its own being as (insofar as it is a "thing") independent of or indifferent to the awareness and the needs of the cognizing organism.

Third (what is actually presupposed in the formulation of the second point), this net of relations (this semiotic web) is woven of threads indifferently real or unreal, only *some of which* (under any given set of circumstances) are in fact realized in the order of *ens reale* as well as objectively within the experience presenting objects here and now considered, but *all of which* are *functionally equivalent* for any prereflexive awareness of objects here and now as this or that (+ or 'to be sought', − or 'to be shunned', Ø or 'safe to ignore').

When these three points are clearly grasped, we are in a position to realize that, while things undoubtedly are more fundamental ontologically than are objects (inasmuch as the latter exist fully as such only within experience, while the former, even when they exist within experience as well, never reduce to the experience in which they are given), from within experience itself objects exist more fundamentally than things, in that the difference between the two is a *discovery to be made*, and a discovery moreover in which we are recurrently mistaken in assigning relative reality or unreality to any given object or aspect of objects under given circumstances.

There are not only honest mistakes, there are also lies believed, both of which can have the direst consequences in the order of *ens reale* for the subjective, physical reality and well being of the organism or organisms involved in the mistake; and whether the mistake is honest or malicious becomes irrelevant. In the animal world without language (the objective world of purely perceptual animals, let us say), there are both prefigurations of art and prefigurations of lies, precisely because every animal is involved in and depends upon a skillful play of real and unreal relations in catching within its net of experience objects it needs to survive and thrive.

10.3. The Distinctiveness of Relations in the Objective World

Now the relations by which objects are constituted in their difference from mere things have two remarkable features which distinguish them from their cousins in the order of *ens reale*, the relations whose whole being as such is intersubjective (and a-fortiori suprasubjective). We have spoken above (pp. 56 and 63) of the 'twofold peculiarity' of relations vis-à-vis the other modes of mind-independent being (i.e., substance and the inherent accidents). But whereas before we were speaking about a twofold peculiarity of relations vis-à-vis the order of *ens reale* as a whole, here we are speaking about a twofold peculiarity of relations wholly *within* the order of objective being, whether it includes *ens reale* in a given case or not. While relations in the order of *ens reale* are in principle dyadic and always intersubjective as well as suprasubjective, relations in the order of *ens obiectivum* are in principle triadic and only sometimes intersubjective as well as suprasubjective. Triadicity and the sometimes-absence of intersubjectivity, thus, are distinctive features of objective relations as such; but it is to be noted that there can be a virtual thirdness, a "degenerate thirdness", as Peirce might say, indirectly at play (a *vis à prospecto* at work) even in the dyadic interactions of inorganic nature.

10.3.1. The first distinctive feature of objectifying relations

The first feature is their triadic character. Physical relations are essentially dyadic in structure or character: there is the individual (the remote fundament) related to another real individual (the terminus) on the basis of this or that of its subjective or "identifying" characteristics (the proximate fundament). But even these same relations dyadic of themselves, when subsumed within experience, acquire a further structural element or feature which distinguishes them as *triadic* in character: there is not only one object standing for or serving to direct attention to yet some other object; there is also the one to or for whom the first object so stands (as I mentioned above without there being able to comment upon it). And just as this third "need not be mental", so the objectivity implied may be virtual rather than actual according to circumstance.

10.3.2. The second distinctive feature of objectifying relations

The second feature is that, while the relations by which objects are constituted are like their dyadic physical cousins always suprasubjective (and hence terminating in principle at objectivity as something 'public' in principle if not always in fact), they are only *sometimes* intersubjective as well; for the action of signs, unlike physical interaction, is not limited to the world of actual physical existence (of "brute Secondness" in the categorial terms of Peirce), even when they do (as they often do) incorporate within the relation triadically signifying dyadic cause-effect relations subsumed from the experience and being of the physical surroundings.

Thus relations in the order of *ens reale* are basically intersubjective: smoke stands to fire as effect to cause. But in the objective order, when smoke comes to be *seen as* a *sign* of fire, a third element has perforce to enter in, namely, *the experience of the organism connecting* smoke with fire; and this connection within experience does not simply reduce to the cause-effect relation obtaining physically prior to and independently of the experience, even though the cause-effect relation is incorporated into the experienced connection (always unconsciously for brute animals, sometimes even consciously by rational animals). If the experience making the connection did simply reduce to the prior dyadic relation of effect to cause, smoke could not be used as a means of communication about other things than fire (as it was used by cowboys and indians alike in the "Wild West" of 18th and 19th century America), nor could smoke sometimes be interpreted rather (not so commonly today as once was the case) as a sign of divine anger, a sign from the gods.

Imagine (not so difficult) the first time smoke appeared in your perception as an object of awareness; and, imagine further, that the billowing smoke was so positioned in your original perceptual field that the fire or combustion generating and connected with it was no part of the perception. *At most*, the smoke *might* (or might not) raise a question in your mind. But basically it would be an *object of experience*, not yet a sign of something burning.

Now: that smoke is not within you, but "in the distance". Yet *something*, a cognitive or psychological state which is other than was your state before becoming aware of the smoke, *is* within you, and *is the basis upon which* the smoke exists for you here and now as an object of awareness.

This psychological condition or state *is not* what you are directly aware of. *Directly*, you are aware of the smoke. *Between* the smoke and your psychological state of awareness is precisely the ever-invisible, intangible, suprasubjective relation at whose term the smoke stands for or represents itself.

This "standing for itself" differentiates the smoke *as an object* from the smoke *as a thing*. As a thing, the smoke does not *stand* for itself; it *is itself*. But as *an object*, the smoke *represents itself* in your awareness. The *awareness* of the smoke, by contrast, does not "stand for" or "represent" itself: it stands for or represents *the object*, which "stands for" itself (not to mention the surrounding cathexis).

But in a little while, let us imagine, you explore the situation; and, soon enough, you come to think that you *see a connection* between smoke and fire. Now the smoke, still an object, is no longer *merely* an object, but *also* a *sign of fire*. As an *object*, the smoke represents only itself. As a *sign*, this object represents not only itself but also something which it itself is not, the fire *as a thing* "causing" the object (also *as a thing*).

10.4. The Distinction Between Objects, Things, and Signs

So we confront once again the difference between objects and things, but now further the difference between objects and signs. On the one hand, things *are* themselves, whereas objects *represent* themselves, factually or fictively. On the other hand, objects represent *themselves* within experience, whereas signs represent always something *other* than themselves, something which they themselves are not; and they do so, these signs, respecting some third element or factor with respect to which the other-representation takes place.

It matters not whether the signs in question (the signs *strictly speaking*, that is to say, the triadic relations upon which objects depend in their essential being as significates) be based on the psychological states of the organism, cathectic and cognitive, or on aspects of objects founding interobjective relations. *In either case*, the elements comprising the sign are three, and the being of the sign as such transcends the three elements by uniting them according to three respective roles, namely: the role of sign-vehicle (the element of other-representation or *representamen*), the role of object signified (the other than the sign-vehicle represented or *significate*), and the role of interpretant (the term to or for which the representation is made).[8]

Thus, while things precede objects as physical environment precedes objective world, things depend upon their incorporation within objects through sensation in order to become known; and objects depend upon the action of signs in order to be at all as cognized. "Significate", in short, says clearly what "object" says obscurely; and "object signified" is actually a redundancy by which the significate is designated in its proper being as dependent upon and derivative from the action of signs.

---

[8] The interpretant is distinct in principle from an *interpreter*, even though, like objects and things, the two may happen to coincide. Thus, in the more obvious cases, representation is made to a person or cognizing organism, but not necessarily in cases we do not have the space here to discuss, exemplified in the contemporary debate over the extent of the action of signs and the notion of physiosemiosis in particular: see Deely 1990: Chap. 6; Nöth 2001; and Deely 2009e.

Chapter 11

The Structure of the Sign

The *structure* of the sign thus is triadic; but the *being* of the sign is the triadic relation itself, not the elements related or structured according to their respective roles,[1] as we have seen. The sign in

---

[1] Special consideration has to be made of the case of so-called "natural signs" in the hardcore sense of a sign which comes to be understood precisely as its other-representative element (the "sign-vehicle" or "representamen") is involved in the 'brute Secondness' of causal interactions (and always allowing for the possibility of being mistaken, as fallibilism requires). Indeed, the Latins had already pointed out that while sign in general consists in a relation indifferently real or unreal ("ontological" in that sense: *relatio secundum esse* — see Poinsot 1632: Book I, Question 1, opening paragraphs), the whole difference between so-called natural signs, on the one hand, and together stipulated and customary signs, on the other hand, lies precisely in the fact that subjective constitution as such enters into the proper signifying of the former but not of the latter signs; yet in neither case does subjective constitution *constitute* the proper signifying. Thus does Poinsot (1632: Book I, Question 2, esp. 137n4) preclude one of the common naive (mis) interpretations of the notion of "natural sign": "those relations by which a sign can be proportioned to a signified are formally other than the sign-relation itself, e.g., the relation of effect to cause, of similitude or image, etc., even though some recent authors confound the sign-relation with these relations, but unwarrantably: because to signify or to be caused or to be similar are diverse exercises in a sign. For in signifying, a substitution for the principal significate is exercised, that that principal may be manifested to a power, but in the rationale of a cause or an effect is included nothing of an order to a cognitive power; wherefore they are distinct fundaments, and so postulate distinct relations. These relations, moreover, can be

its proper being is superordinate to its subordinate elements, to all three of the "terms" of every sign relation. And which subordinate

---

separated from the sign-relation, just as a son is similar to the father and his effect and image, but not a sign. The sign-relation therefore adds to these relations, which it supposes or prerequires in order to be habilitated and proportioned to this significate rather than to that one." See further Book I, Question 3, 160/10–21; and cf. the discussion in note 13 of that same Question, pp. 163–164.

Whence one and the same "sign" — a volcano, say, erupting, seen by the scientist as a release of pressure and shift of plates within the earth, seen by a local primitive tribe as a manifestation of divine wrath — can function in one perspective "naturally" and in another perspective "arbitrarily": Poinsot 1632: *Tractatus de Signis*, Book II, Question 6, "Utrum signum ex consuetudine sit vere signum", 282/23–283/22: "it is not antinomic that two ways of signifying should attach to the same thing according to distinct formalities. Whence, when one mode of signifying is removed, the other remains; and so the same sign is never a natural sign and a stipulated sign formally, even though a natural and a stipulated sign may be the same materially, that is, even though a natural and a stipulated mode of signifying may belong to the same subject." And the same must be said of representamens established by custom.

Here is worth repeating the point from Deely 2005b:1 9n11: Indeed, the Latins had already pointed out that while sign in general consists in a relation indifferently real or unreal ("ontological" in that sense: *relatio secundum esse* — See Poinsot 1632: Book I, Question 1, opening paragraphs), the whole difference between so-called natural signs, on the one hand, and together stipulated and customary signs, on the other hand (i.e., signs in the sense identified by Saussure as 'arbitrary'), lies precisely in the fact above noted that subjective constitution as such enters into the proper signifying of the former but not of the latter signs. Hence, by assimilating the account of natural signs to his stipulated paradigm, Saussure eliminated the zoösemiotic component of human communication in a manner exactly paralleling Descartes' elimination of animality from the essential definition of the human being.

Yet even for the conventional signs of human language, stipulation is not the whole story. Social interaction among animals, *nonhuman as well as human*, establishes signs which are "arbitrary" from the point of view of their subjective components (the *signifié* as concept and the *signifiant* as acoustic image, for example), yet are wholly based on habit establishment ('*ex consuetudine*') without any involvement of stipulation. In the human case stipulation *can* always enter in; but the point is that it *does not in fact* always enter in, and that is precisely the zone where zoösemiosis finds its place in human experience exactly as it does in the social experience of nonhuman animal interaction.

The study of this component in human language (of the *signum ex consuetudine* in contrast to the *signum ad placitum*) has largely been ignored in the modern period. The only contemporary author I know of who has thematically studied human discourse from the point of view precisely of the *ex consuetudine* element of convention (based in principle on collective behavior alone) *in its difference* from the *ad* element is which is determined primarily by its position or role within the triadic relation and only secondarily, if at all (for many signs have no "hardcore" reality component to speak of), by anything intrinsic to the element as subjectively constituted.

The element in the foreground of representation is the *sign-vehicle*, what is loosely and commonly called a "sign", and which can be pointed to or seen or heard when it occurs outside the psychology (the subjective states) of the organism. The element itself represented (the "self-representation" in contrast with the "other-representation" of the 'representamen' or sign-vehicle) is the *object signified*[2] or significate, which is represented in or by the sign-vehicle; and the one to or for which the representation of sign to signified is accomplished Peirce called "the Interpretant", in order to make the point that it need not be a person or even mental, which point, as I have had reluctantly to say already, is out of bounds for the present discussion.

In this way it can be seen that objects, normally confused with things by human animals, are not only distinct in principle from (while yet always partially involving) things; but that objects also (what is far from evident, and indeed quite surprising) actually *presuppose signs **in order to be objects in the first place**.* And objects presuppose signs no less in order *subsequently* (experientially speaking) to be distinguished from things in the course of experience. Indeed, the experience of the difference between things and objects

---

placitum element (based in principle on collective behavior as *further fixed* by rule) is Keller (see Keller 1994 and 1998). When Saussure's perspective is modified by the kind of results Keller achieves, his model, though remaining anthropocentric, is yet opened on the margins to zoösemiosis as realized within anthroposemiosis — precisely the opening that Sebeok exploited in Lotman's work (Deely 2009e: 171n7), but without ever having made even initially the blunder of thinking that the relation involved in signification for arbitrary signs could properly be anything other than an irreducible triad adding *significatum* to *significant* and *signifié*. See further Deely 2009: 86n30 (in Section 9.7) and 92n42 (in Section 9.8); and Deely 2009d.

[2] Notice the redundancy here, for there is no other type of object than one *signified* — so that, in short, to speak of an *object* and to speak of a *significate* are one and the same "speaking". Concealed in the word 'object' is always a significate, but far from always a thing.

provides (from within the species-specifically human awareness of being) what Aquinas calls its "first division",[3] to wit, the contrast within the objective world between what does and what does not reduce to our experience of relatives fashioned by the cognitive organism — the contrast between the opposed orders of *ens reale*, on the one hand, and *ens rationis*, on the other hand.

11.1. What Perception Hides

In pure perception this distinction is entirely hidden. Perception yields only an objective world structured along the lines of +, −, 0; that is all. Of course mistakes are possible. The animal that

---

[3] Aquinas c.1268/72: *In IV Met.*, lect. 3, n. 3: "unum quod cum ente convertitur importat privationem divisionis formalis quae fit per opposita, cuius prima radix est oppositio affirmationis et negationis. Nam illa dividuntur adinvicem, quae ita se habent, quod hoc non est illud. Primo igitur intelligitur ipsum ens, *et ex consequenti non ens*, et per consequens divisio, et per consequens unum quod divisionem privat, et per consequens multitudo, in cuius ratione cadit divisio, sicut in ratione unius indivisio; quamvis aliqua divisa modo praedicto rationem multitudinis habere non possint nisi prius cuilibet divisorum ratio unius attribuatur." — "the sense of 'one' which is convertible with being imports the privative absence of a formal division which comes about through opposites, the first root of which is the opposition of affirmation and of negation. For those things are reciprocally divided which are so related that this one is not that one. Therefore being itself is first understood, *and nonbeing only as a consequence*, and through this consequence division, and the unity or 'one' which division deprives, and consequently multitude in the rationale of which falls division, just as in the rationale of the one falls indivision; although any things divided in the aforesaid manner could not have the rationale of a multitude unless the rationale of unity had already been attributed to each member of the multitude." (Cf. Aristotle c.BC 348/7: *Metaphysics*, Book III, 1001a3–b26, esp. at 1001b6–7: "The world is either one or many; but if many, each of the many must be a one".)

As Poinsot summarily puts the point (1632: 51/3–6): "in hoc consistit habere esse objective in intellectu, id est ex ipso modo cognoscendi affici apprehensive ut ens, quod non est ens." — "in this consists the having of being objectively in the understanding, to wit, from the very mode of cognizing to be affected apprehensively as being that which is not being." The procedure is actually common to all animals capable of *phantasiari*, but only those animals — semiotic animals, in effect, animals capable, beyond *phantasiari*, of *intelligere* — are able to see the procedure for what it is, namely, the root of the difference between objects and things (Poinsot 1632: 66/46–68/35). See Deely 2009: 79, Section 9.3., and note 1 of this chapter, for further references and discussion on this point. Also Deely 2007.

miscalculates loses its prey and starves. The prey that misreads the signs and takes a "minus" object for a "zero" object falls prey and is eaten. Deceit and camouflage are resorted to throughout the animal kingdom, and even among plants, as it happens. But, just as we cannot go into the story of physiosemiosis here, so too that of phytosemiosis.

Here, the point is that the objective world, *the primary reality for every animal as such*, is the world of objects ready-to-hand, the objective world or Umwelt, the world wherein the physical environment does not merely exist but *so exists* as to support in sensation a network of perceptual relations which reveal an objective *meaning* in the otherwise subjective realm of physical being with its dyadic *intersubjective* relations in principle indifferent to the differences of lifeforms. The relations themselves (*both* the purely objective ones *and* the ones objective as well as physical) the animal without language does not perceive, only the related objects with which it needs to deal in getting on with life, i.e., the objects presented as terminating the relations of sense-perception interpreting and structuring the data of sensation as such to constitute the Umwelt, the objective world of what is to be sought, what avoided, and what safe to ignore.

The reason for the obliviousness to relations in their difference from the objects related on the part of organism perceiving is quite simple. Whereas the related objects normally include, through sensation, a subjective physical dimension objectified, these very objects, in their subjectivity and intersubjectivity objectified (their character as "real"), can be seen, felt, touched, and eaten. They can be pointed to, stalked, tricked, played with. But what makes locating them, stalking them, deceiving them, possible in the first place is not something that appears to the senses: it is the way the sought (or shunned) objects are situated and manipulated within a network of relations at once real and unreal according to the requirements of the situations — that structured objective being alone, not the relations by which it is experientially sustained and without which it would not appear as structured, is what appears to the senses.

11.2. What Objectivity Requires

The sustaining relations, the very fabric of objectivity as developed within and carried by the experience of the individual organism, are not objects directly perceived or perceivable. The objects directly perceived are the *termini* of cognitive relations, whether these termini be things as well (such as once was Napoleon) or whether these termini be only objects from the beginning (such as remains Hamlet). Normally, as we have seen, objects are a mixture of *ens reale* and *ens rationis*; but not always, and not necessarily.

It matters not whether a sense-perception be mistaken or veridical. In either case, the object presented and apprehended exists as a significate, purely objective in the respect in which the perception is mistaken, physical *as well* as objective in the respect in which the perception is veridical. The action wherein and whereby the objects are presented here and now is semiosis, and the relations whereby the objects are presented here and now are triadic, that is to say, sign relations. These triadic relations, wholly invisible to sense (external or internal), are the being which makes the sign be a sign.

The representative element within this triadic structure, which we loosely call a "sign", "in itself" is *not a sign at all*, but one of the three elements *necessary to the being of a sign*, one of the three legs on which the sign walks in working its way through the world, and, indeed, the "foremost" leg, insofar as it is the leg which takes the direct representative step carrying a semiosis. What is sign-vehicle one time can be significate another time; and what is interpretant one time can be sign-vehicle the next time; and so on, in an unending spiral — an "unlimited semiosis", as Peirce is reputed as having liked to say — of abductions, deductions, and retroductions through and over the course of which "symbols grow", thus:[4]

---

[4] "Spiral of Semiosis" diagram, originally in Deely 1985a, subsequently reproduced in Deely 2001a: 28; 2003: 164; 2009: Section 15.5, toward the end. Please note that the term "retroduction", though taken from Peirce materially, bears in my work a stipulated sense of the Latin *descensus* from concepts to things rather than the sense of the Latin *ascensus* (or "abduction") stipulated by Peirce, with the rationale of the shift fully explained in 2009: Section 15.5, 167–169, esp. 167n4.

**The Semiotic Spiral, where A = abduction,
B = deduction, C = retroduction**

11.3. *What Modern Epistemologies Miss*

If modern philosophy depends upon an epistemological paradigm which knows no path beyond the representative contents of consciousness, while epistemology constitutes for semiotics no more than its "midmost target",[5] the reason is that study of the action of signs finds precisely a path beyond the representative contents of consciousness: *renvoi*, as Jakobson termed it,[6] the "Way of Signs". For the "contents of consciousness" are not self-representations (objects) but, precisely, themselves signs (other-representations)[7] rooted in the being of triadic relations which transcend the divisions between nature and culture, inner and outer. Whence, *pace* Descartes, the "*passiones animae*"[8] — the "passions of the soul", or (in modern parlance) psychological states of the animal — as provenating necessarily in *their* distinctive being relations terminating objectively, sustain objects which cannot be confined *any more than can relation itself* to either side of any *ens reale/ens rationis*, objectivity/ subjectiviy divide, real or imagined, notwithstanding the indubitable "subjectivity" of the psychological states themselves as qualities

---

[5] Sebeok 1991: 2.

[6] Jakobson 1974; Deely 1993a, together with the further revision proposed in Deely 2001c: 721–722. See gloss on this entry in the References to this volume.

[7] The point is fundamental: cf. Poinsot 1632: 117/12–17. Cf. the discussion of the status of the representamen in Deely 2003: 6–7 text & note 4, 28, 76, 197–198, 200–203.

[8] Cf. Descartes 1649; Deely 2009d.

within *ens reale* provenating relations irreducible to intersubjectivity restrictively conceived as *ens reale*.

The "central preoccupation" of semiotics may be, à la modernity, "an illimitable array of concordant illusions", Sebeok reported to the Semiotic Society of America in his Presidential Address of 1984, but "its main mission" — its postmodern task, as we may say — is "to mediate [even a mixed success is better than none] between reality and illusion."

Chapter 12

At the Turn of the 21st Century: The New Definition of Human Being Beyond Patriarchy and Feminism

Sebeok liked to say that semiosis was criterial of life, and even that sign-science and life-science are therefore coextensive. The "therefore" does not follow, I have argued; but semiosis is certainly criterial of life, if not in the sense that semiosis occurs *only* among the living, at least in the sense that life without semiosis is rather death, quite impossible to sustain. Of all living things we can say that they are semiosic creatures, creatures which grow and develop through the manipulation of sign-vehicles and the involvement in sign-processes, semiosis. If this is true of all the living, a-fortiori is it true of all animals: every animal is a semiosic animal, able to survive and thrive only thanks to whatever semiosic competence it is able to manage.

What, then, distinguishes the human being among the other animals? It is not by any means semiosis, as we have seen. What distinguishes the human being among the animals on earth is quite simple, yet was never fully grasped before modern times had reached the state of Latin times in the age of Galileo. While every animal of necessity *makes use* of signs, yet because signs themselves consist in relations, and because every relation, real or unreal, is *as relation* — as a suprasubjective orientation toward something other than the

one oriented, be that "other" purely objective or subjective as well
— invisible to sense (and hence can be directly *understood* in its difference from related objects or things, but can never be directly *perceived* as such), what distinguishes the human being from the other
animals is that *only human animals* come to realize that *there are* signs
distinct from and superordinate to every particular thing that serves
to constitute an individual (including the material structure of an
individual sign-vehicle) in its distinctness from its surroundings.

Just as objects are distinct in principle from things, so signs are
in principle distinct from objects. Just as the understanding species-
specific to human animals can penetrate beyond the sensible aspects
of objects to inquire into their constitution as things existing independently of relations they happen to have with us in cognition,
so the understanding species-specific to humans can recognize the
difference between the *triadic relation*, which makes a sign-vehicle
function as an other-representation within semiosis, and the *sign-
vehicle* itself in its subjective or "real" being, material (as in the case
of a sound or mark) or psychological (as in the case of an idea or
feeling) or purely objective (as in the case of Camelot as a symbol of
King Arthur's court). Nominalism, the claim that there are only particulars, is falsified by the being proper to signs. *This* being, the being
proper to signs, realest of the real as constituting the experiences
themselves within which being is experienced in whatever way, is
not that of a particular, a subjectivity identifiable objectively among
other subjectivities. On the contrary, the being proper to signs is the
being of a suprasubjective and triadic means of union wherein and
whereby one "thing" can come to stand for another, real or unreal
— which depending upon circumstances that can be investigated on
the side of things as such only by an animal capable of distinguishing
relations as such (objective only or intersubjective as well as suprasubjective) from "*related things*" or (if you prefer) "*objects experienced*".

Such an animal, capable of coming to know that there are signs
as well as of using signs to hunt and fish and find its way through
the surroundings, is generically semiosic but specifically semiotic,
that is to say, is the only animal capable of knowing that there are

signs to be studied as well as made use of to more "practical" ends. So a definition of the human being as "semiotic animal" is not modern. In the modern understanding of the philosophers, *ens reale* went under erasure, while *ens rationis*, mind-dependent being, came to be the whole of objectivity.

With Peirce's New List of Categories this epistemologically closed situation of modern philosophy (in principle, not in sociological fact, of course) came definitively to closure. For what the New List essayed was a scheme wherein the fabric of experience as an interweave of relations at once real and unreal together (and which shifting according to circumstances, as the being of relation indifferently in the orders of *ens reale* and *ens rationis* uniquely and singularly allows) sustains the experience of all objects as such and explains the possibilities equally of truth and error in our interpretations of "things". The New List was a semiotic list, the first attempt of semiotic consciousness to reclassify being from within experience as just what it cenoscopically seems to be: a confused and confusing mixture of *ens reale* and *ens rationis*. This new approach was no mere return to a medieval scheme of realism, wherein relations as intersubjectivities are recognized along with subjectivities in the list of Aristotelian categories (the attempt to classify the ways in which being can be verified existing independently of the cognitive activity of our minds), though it includes such a return. The new approach is, at the same time, and most importantly, a move beyond the frontier of idealism that modernity circumscribed in the separation of philosophy from science, a move beyond the frontier defined as forever unpassable in Kant's 1783 *Prolegomenon to Any Future Metaphysics*.

For the action of signs surpasses that frontier, and the study of signs, *eo ipso*, is carried by that action consequently beyond that frontier deemed by modern philosophy to be unpassable. That is why the understanding and definition of the human being reached by the study of semiosis, the way of signs, floresces early into an understanding and definition of the human being that is as distinctively *postmodern* as the modern definition of the human being as a "thinking thing" was distinctively *postmedieval*. With the definition of the human being among the animals as the only *semiotic animal* — that is to say, the only animal capable of recognizing that there are signs (as distinct from their practical recognition and use) and capable of developing accordingly a semiotic consciousness of the radical role played by signs as well in the inescapable realism of animals as in the growth of all experience and of human understanding in particular, with its symbols everywhere in culture — we locate ourselves along a way of signs which leads "everywhere in nature, including those domains where humans have never set foot".[1]

Semiotics recovers the *ens reale* insisted upon as knowable by scholastic realism; yet, at the same time, semiotics demonstrates the objectivity of *ens rationis* in the social construction of species-specific realities among biological organisms. With this twofold accomplishment, semiotics manifests the distinctiveness of cultural reality in the human species as the *locus* where the differences between *ens reale* and *ens rationis* become knowable and distinguishable as such consequent upon the human grasp of *ens primum cognitum*. The spirit of ancient and medieval "realism" is recovered and vindicated, while at the same time it is surpassed as necessary but not sufficient to grasp the human condition and the project of philosophy as cœnoscopic science. Semiotics achieves not a return but an advance, the opening of a new era of intellectual culture, for philosophy first of all, to be sure, but also for science and the humanities, wherein the split between nature and culture, inner and outer, self and other, is no longer the last word, because the quasi-fallacy of the external world has finally been laid to rest, and with it modern philosophy.

We are, as it were, in a position to say to the epoch of modernity in philosophy what the early moderns said so emphatically to the epoch of medieval thought: *Requiescat in pace*. The postmodern development of the self-understanding of the semiotic animal implies no less.

---

[1] Emmeche 1994: 126.

And notice this. As a definition, semiotic animal, no less than "animal rationale" or "res cogitans", shows what *sets the human being apart* within nature, but, at the same time, and in contrast to both earlier definitions, it *shows that what sets us apart is an awareness of the very process that ties us into nature as a whole*. "Rational animal" did not do this, for "rational" showed only what sets us apart in the sense of "above" the rest of animal nature. It played into the false hierarchy of nature from the lowest substances susceptible of corruption to the higher substances immune to substantial change to the highest substances, the "Separated Intelligences" or "angels" who move the sun and stars governing all generations and corruptions (all substantial changes) in the sphere below the moon. "Res cogitans" did the same, in the sense of placing the human being simply above all material interactions of things. "Semiotic animal" effects no such separation, but rather underlines the continuity whereby, in semiosis, all lifeforms, including humans, "live and move and have their being". *What distinguishes the semiotic animal is the awareness of what ties its being in with the whole of nature*, what makes it a part of the unfolding cosmic whole.

The most important feature of the rational animal was the feature that set it *above* the rest of animal nature, and *apart* from material nature as a whole; and both of these points pertain also, especially the latter point, to the 'thinking thing' contrasted with the '*res extensae*', that physical environment we call "the universe". From its Aristotelian roots, we should further note, this way of defining the human being as "separate" within nature grew into the tree of patriarchy setting "man" above "woman" as the supposedly *more rational* by reason of bodily type. Modern feminism challenged patriarchy, mainly by claiming that woman could act in the public sphere equally with men. Later feminists claimed to be rather "postmodern", in the literary sense associated with 20ᵗʰ century "semiology",[2] by treating dismissively the reality of subjectivity in favor of 'relationalism'.

---

[2] The work of Kristeva falls wholly here. See Sebeok 1996: 54, cited in note 20 of the *Sequel* on semioethics, p. 118 below. Cf. Deely 1986a; 1990: Chap. 1;

Semiotic animal, by contrast, serves "to call into question older paradigms (premodern and modern) of patriarchy and feminism that alike prove to be inadequate for developing thought",[3] since semiotic animal provides in the spiral of abductions "lived testimony of a semiotic reality beyond the gender trap of both 'patriarchy' and 'feminism',"[4] — a trap Williams well describes as "those historically inherited dualisms that signified the male human being as the absolute measure of a 'rational animal'."[5] This surprising implication of the definition of human as "semiotic animal" first came to my attention in Williams' discussion of a "time for a semiosis beyond feminism".[6] Semiotics, as the postmodern turn or era of philosophical development, with its accompanying definition (or redefinition) of human beings as "semiotic animals", she remarked,[7] "opens the way of perfection not only beyond the Western intellectual tradition's concept of woman as less perfect than man,[8] but also beyond the modern semiotic of feminism." Understanding the human being as semiotic animal leads us "in the direction of a new paradigm, both inclusive of and beyond sex differentiation", and surely exclusive of "domination"!

2001: Chaps. 15 and 16.

   [3] Williams Deely 2008: 43.

   [4] Ibid. 44.

   [5] Ibid. 41.

   [6] This was in her paper presented 18 October 2008 at the 33rd Annual Meeting of the Semiotic Society of America, and since published in the *Semiotics 2008* Proceedings volume of that year.

   [7] Ibid. 44.

   [8] This is a tradition in the so-called "West", indeed, especially in the Islamic parts (see Deely 2001: Chap. 1, esp. as summarized later in note 53, pp. 189–190, however, on the proper notion of philosophy as *neither* "Eastern" *nor* "Western"); but the pattern of domination in question is hardly distinctively "Western" — where, indeed, in (very) late modern Europe and the Americas at least, this invidious "tradition" has been much ameliorated — and is rooted in the original "division of labor" imposed on primitive humans by the consequences of pregnancy in childbearing. This is a story too far afield from the present work, which, however, I hope to take up jointly with Williams in a commentary on Mill's 1869 classic on *The Subjection of Women.*

There is a rational mode of knowing, indeed, that is distinctive of anthroposemiosis. But that mode is no more than a mode, a mode embedded along with many other modes, both some distinctive of and others not distinctive of yet all essential to anthroposemiosis in its own right. I have in mind those modes of cathexis and also cognition where zoösemiosis overlaps with and makes possible in the first place anthroposemiosis as a *further* development species-specific in type — including those bodily modes without which anthroposemiosis would collapse like a house of cards, fall as flat as a balloon without air. Even should the rational soul survive bodily death,[9] still it would not transcend semiosis, any more than pure spirits — angels — can have knowledge independently of the action of signs.[10]

The semiotic animal in semiosis at once involves and transcends gender, just as it at once involves and transcends *ens reale*, for the very same reason that it does *not* transcend the biosphere. The "mode of knowing" distinctive overall of the semiotic animal is suprarational, accordingly (that is, inclusive of but not wholly reducible to the rational), even as the action of signs is suprasubjective. "Nature for man", in Messner's famous formula,[11] we discover to be care for the whole of earthly life (perhaps one day even beyond), no less than is "nature for woman"; and "rationality" for every human being is properly at the service, in the indirect particulars of daily life, of that "good of the whole" on which each specific part depends — semiotic animals no less than the other animals, because all animals are, along with plants and nature itself, semiosic in being! The contemplative tradition, where care depends upon understanding's seeing of the whole, and follows from it, proves to be the current underlying that overall movement of and development within nature that we call "anthroposemiosis", the human use of signs available only to animals able manipulate relations in their

---

[9] See the "Appendix on Immortality" in Deely 2009c: 87–90.

[10] See Deely 2004c, "The Semiosis of Angels", entirely based on Aquinas and Poinsot.

[11] Messner 1965: 44.

singular being transcendent to the being of related things knowable in their own right through acting according to what they are.

Sequel

The Ethical Entailment
of Semiotic Animal, or the
Need to Develop a Semioethics

"Dicitur in iii de anima, quod intellectus speculativus per exten-
sionem fit practicus. una autem potentia non mutatur in aliam. ergo
intellectus speculativus et practicus non sunt diversae potentiae."

Thomas Aquinas 1266: Q. 79, Art. 11, sed contra

"In his treatment of the human soul Aristotle remarks that specula-
tive understanding by extension becomes practical. But one cognitive
power does not change into another one. Thus speculative and practical
understanding are achievements of the intellect as one same power."

"Modern man" can indeed be said to have been "the animal
that does not want to be an animal",[1] that did not admit to its animality (at least not in its fullness, if at all), preferring[2] "a Cartesian
dualism between culture and nature which has opposed humans
to the rest of the natural world for centuries". Of course, modern
man to the end adhered to the illusion that "man" is a sufficiently
comprehensive linguistic expression to designate the human species
of animal as a whole, male or female!

---

[1] Tønnessen 2003: 287.

[2] Nöth 2001: 283.

1. Rethinking the Relation of Civilization to Nature

Postmodern awareness of humanity within nature and among the forms of animal life *begins* at a level beyond all that, as we have seen; and just as the semiotic animal sees a way beyond the modern impasse of idealism vs. realism and the *ne plus ultra* of Kantian epistemology, so at the same time does it awaken to the need for a deeper notion of person than "supposit (or 'individual substance') of a rational nature". For the semiotic self is not reducible to the categories of individual subjectivity within a species. The "irreducible surplus" of which Pope John Paul II speaks in connection with the notion of the human person[3] is precisely the product of semiosis at work among the human animals — anthroposemiosis — at one and the same time bringing about the fulfillment of their unique capacities of cathexis and cognition, and tying them into the biosphere and the whole of physical nature as providing (largely beyond the margins of consciousness, to be sure) the developmental framework for the very possibility of anthroposemiosis in the first place.

The modern treatment of ethics, accordingly — that is to say, the ethical discourse to which we have become accustomed, especially in the wake of the pathological "linguistic turn" within the Analytic tradition — requires its own transformative assimilation to befit the postmodern context. Nor is the *point de depart* for this assimilation of philosophy's past (not only modernity! but the middle Latin and ancient Greek ages as well) far to seek. It must surely be in the development of Hoffmeyer's distinction, taken up by Tønnessen,[4] between "moral subject" and "moral agent", which

---

[3] Wojtyła 1978: 110, cited p. 116 below. Cf. Maritain 1947, a book quite controversial in its time precisely because it did not easily fit the established "metaphysical" perspectives of Neothomistic "realism".

[4] Hoffmeyer 1993: 152–176, esp. 164–166 (= 151–153 in the 1995 reprint) "Biosemiotics and the Question of Moral Subjects"; see further Tønnessen 2003, *passim*. Tønnessen's expressed reservation concerning Hoffmeyer's foundation, however (2003: 284n2), speaks rather in Hoffmeyer's favor than toward the narrower ethical purview that Tønnessen proposes. Both Hoffmeyer and Tønnessen draw in this discussion from Jon Wetlesen 1993. The point seems to be one coming

at once enables and *requires* the postmodern thinker to extend the notion of a "right to moral consideration" on the part of moral agents *beyond* the realm of human interactions within culture to include the larger biosphere presupposed to very existence and healthy development of (as Sebeok put it[5]) "that minuscule segment of nature" modern thought has tended to "grandly compartmentalize as culture".

Every species is semiosic; but only a species that is semiotic as well as semiosic is bound to "go global", as the only species whose individual members exercise moral agency as part and parcel inescapably of their subjectivity. Respecting such a species, however long the realization may take to dawn, responsibility, implicitly global, become explicitly so when the scientific development of ideoscopy reaches a critical "tipping point", such as we are witnessing in the turn-of-the-21st-century *climate destabilization* brought about by technology and commonly (if somewhat discombobulatively) termed "global warming".

But let us not get too far ahead of the story.

2. The Modern Impasse in Its Origins

A semiotic animal is an animal that lives with the awareness that the action of signs is more fundamental to the constitution of human experience than are either objects or things. Philosophical *idealism* in the modern sense began with the realization that objects cannot actually exist as such save in relation to a knower, a "thinking thing". If human beings are the only animals that think, then "thinking thing", exactly as Descartes proposed, is the proper

---

into general recognition. Thus Arne Johan Vetlesen (1994: 3), announcing that he restricts "discussion of 'morality' to what obtains — or fails to obtain — between human subjects", yet asks the reader to "note that this does not imply that I hold only humans to have a moral standing". In the semioethic view — that is, a view of ethics stringently derived from semiosis itself precisely as involving the human — morality cannot be restricted only to what obtains or not between human subjects, but concerns also the actions and impact of human subjects upon the environment itself, both physical, biological, social, and cultural.

[5] Sebeok 1985a: 2.

definition of the human being in its species-specific uniqueness, and all the rest are mere bodies, "extended things". Against this modern dawning, philosophical *realism* continued to insist on the priority of things over objects, because things do not have to be thought in order to be. But things do have to be thought in order to be known; and so began the long struggle, in all its variations, between "realism", on the one hand, insisting on the knowable reality of things which need not be thought in order to be (and which constitute an order without which there could be no thinkers at all), and "idealism", on the other hand, insisting on the relation to the knower as that without which nothing could either be or be known as far as philosophers, those "thinking things", are concerned.

3. The Achilles Heel of Modern Philosophy

Yet this inevitable and inescapable "relation to a knower" which gave to idealism, as Heidegger put it (1927: 251), "no matter how contrary and untenable" its results, "an advantage in principle", proved also to be an Achilles Heel. For when thought fastened onto this relation as a thematic focus,[6] what soon enough appeared was the discovery that nothing about the relationship itself characterized it intrinsically as belonging exclusively either to mind or to nature. The relationship manifested itself rather as open to both in a manner *indifferent to their difference* as provenating on the one hand an experience of objects which involve also things and on the other hand objects whose being reduced to their apprehension and social acceptance. In other words, the necessity of the relation to a cognitive organism upon which idealism rightly insisted, and which realism tried to marginalize, turned out to be the root of the prior possibility of an action of signs upon which all experience of objects and/or things of nature depends.[7] What never occurred to either the modern idealists or realists over the long course of their

---

[6] Poinsot 1632, *Tractatus de Signs*, Book I, Question 1, "Utrum signum sit in genere relationis".

[7] Cf. ibid., Second Preamble "On Relation", Art. 2, 93/17–96/36.

debate was that the priority for establishing awareness of whatever
kind belongs neither to objects nor to things but to signs as triadic
ontological relations, suprasubjective in principle as relations and
triadic in their character as semiosic relations, that is to say, the relations consequent upon the action of signs.[8]

Of course, we should not oversimplify the situation. Sign relations, which is to say, signs in their proper being as signs, are not
free-floating entities pure and simple. They need to be grounded,
and grounded moreover in three terms simultaneously in order to
achieve their proper significate outcome.[9] The relation itself constituting the sign is always and necessarily suprasubjective in character,
but the foundation or "*sign-vehicle*", the representamen, from which
the sign points to its *object signified*, may be objective only or subjective as well, and the one to or for whom the sign-vehicle presents
the object signified as other than itself, the *interpretant*, need not be
a cognitive power or organism (although it is easiest to understand
the role of the interpretant in cases where it is — Peirce called it
"a sop to Cerberus"). Nor need the interpretant even be actual
but only virtual, as often occurs in physiosemiosis, particularly in
the early phases prior to life where the future influences the past
through the present sufficiently to bring it about that events move
in the direction of the emergence of living things and the beginnings of biosemiosis.

4. The Extent of Semiosis

Let us think a moment over the long span of that semiosis
whereby first the stars and planets form and then, upon the planets,
some of them at least — though how many at the moment we can
only guess (knowing but the one instance of our own world for
sure "as a matter of fact", while suspecting *many* more as a matter
of principle and overwhelming probability) — comes forth life. As

---

[8] Ibid., Book I, Question 3. "Whether the relation of sign to signified is the
same as the relation of sign to cognitive power".

[9] Peirce 1905/6: CP 5.473. Deely 1990: Chap. 3.

soon as we cross that threshold we are into the realm no longer of pure *physiosemiosis* with its virtualities but into the sphere of biosemiosis, the activities of life within organisms which depends at every step on *communication* mediated by signs, that is to say, upon semiosis, between the organisms and their environment and the organisms with one another. Sebeok, who did more than anyone else to establish this concept of the semiosis coextensive with the boundaries of life itself, "biosemiosis", had many terms to describe its lower reaches among the eukaryotes, prokaryotes, and bacteria (*microsemiotics*), fungi and slime molds (*mycosemiotics*), as well as within the higher organisms (including ourselves) whose maintenance of self-identity as individual substances depends intimately on our hosting of colonies and varieties of other organisms within our very bodies (*endosemiotics*). I do not mean to oversimplify the complexities of this grand biosemiosis, so well developed in our recent understanding in particular by the subsequent works of Hoffmeyer, Kull, Emmeche, Markoš, etc. Yet it may be enough for my purposes, in this highly restricted purview, to speak of biosemiosis simply in terms of *phytosemiosis*, covering the action of signs among plants and between plants and animals insofar as the semiosis originates on the side of the plants; *zoösemiosis*, covering the action of signs among animals (including their reaction to phytosemioses) apart from language; and *anthroposemiosis*, covering the human use of signs both overlapping with, but especially as species-specifically distinct from, zoösemiosis.

In phytosemiosis there is little in the way of choice. It is not a question of stimulus-response, however, but of a truly triadic interaction subsuming dyadicity that sustains the life of plants,[10] as we witness for example in the trees uninfected that develop the same antibodies through communication with the tree that is infected. In zoösemiosis, by contrast, we enter the realm of animals and the Umwelt properly conceived as such. For only in the life of animals do things fully become objects, and objects become cathected and

---

[10] Krampen 1981; Deely 1982b, and 1990: Chap. 6.

constructed according to the lifeplan of the animals as + (to be sought), − (to be avoided), and Ø (safely to be ignored).

In the Umwelt of the animal, the idealist "relation to the knower" is not only the key, it is everything. The world of objects cathected and constructed on the animal's lifeplan is, like every objective world, a mixture of relations mind-independent and mind-dependent, an "intersection of nature and culture" *in virtuo*, as it were, inasmuch as every system of orientation to and within an environment requires the formation of relations which have no being apart from the cognizing of the organism.[11] Yet the organism cognizing has no interest in the matter apart from the object that the system of orientation enables it to seek or avoid. If the relations were not in sufficient measure mind-independent, the organism would starve or be eaten. If the relations were not in sufficient measure mind-dependent, the organism would not be able to find its way in the environment — toward what it seeks, or away from what it seeks to avoid. But, beyond the seeking or the avoiding, the organism has no interest, no interest whatever. That the relations succeed in forming a semiotic web catching the prey and eluding the enemy is all that counts. End of story.

More than this. The *things related*, that is to say, in the case before us, the *object or objects signified*, are accessible to sense perception. The relations which constitute them as objects cathected and constructed as +, −, or Ø, however, make no direct entry into the equation. The relations as such, the relations as suprasubjective strands of the web within which objects exist incorporating things interpreted in this or that fashion, are essential to what the organism perceives, but they are "in themselves" of no interest at all to the organism. The organism is interested in *what is interpreted*, the objects signified, not at all in *what makes the interpretation possible in the first place*, be it the internal constitution of things in the physical environment prior to interpretation or the semiosic web of sign relations respecting which the objects themselves (like the organism

---

[11] See Deely 2001, 2001b, and 2002.

perceiving) are comparatively *subjective*. And they must be subjective as well as objective most of the time, at least, in the case of the + objects; otherwise, the animals would die of starvation.

5. The Animal Which Would Become Semiotic

Enter among the animals, now, what Aristotle in his *Politics* called the ζῷον λογον ἐχῶν, the animal capable of communicating linguistically, which would become — as I now think, with some impoverishment — the *rational animal* of Porphyry's tree (c.271AD) and of medieval philosophy, the animal "capable of reasoning" intellectually. Such an animal, and such an animal alone among the lifeforms of planet earth, is *capable* of knowing *that* there are signs, and (quite a further step again) *what* signs are. Yet such an animal is not yet the same as a semiotic animal.

A semiotic animal is not an animal merely *capable* of knowing that there are signs, in distinction from objects and things. That is a rational animal, presupposed and essential to but not yet constitutive of that same animal as semiotic. The semiotic animal emerges only as the *realization* of the capacity of the rational animal for "perceiving the relation of signification" (Maritain 1957: 53). Such an animal belongs to a different level of actualization, a level at which the individual human being has achieved a personal identity inseparable from his or her experiences of things other than the self, including both others that are other human selves, and others that are selves but not human selves, and others that are not selves at all but part of or hostile to the self that is experiencing. Yet the whole of this "self and others" involving my self, this irreducible layer of experience bound up with my being as a web which the individual centers, results in quite another self than the biological organism constituting an individual as human (or not). This "other self", as Dr. Petrilli said in Vienna,[12] "presents a surplus, something more with respect to identity itself, which it transcends", and transcends in the direction of other bodies, objects all insofar as they

---

[12] Petrilli 2003: 112.

are known, whatever their biological and physical status. The correlation of Innenwelt to Umwelt is essential to the semiotic animal.

Thus the semiotic animal is considerably more than the rational animal. The rational animal is a type of substance, an individual of a species. The semiotic animal is a self, unique within the species of which it yet forms an individual instance. The semiotic animal is aware of its world, yet it is no mere *res cogitans*, for it is bound up from the first with a surrounding environment and world concerning which, little by little, it grasps the "reasons for being" (not without mistakes, of course). Rationality is a *capacity* for reasonableness, quite compatible as such with a *res cogitans*. Yet this same capacity viewed in the context of a semiotic animal cannot be separated from "the ability to grasp the reason *of things*",[13] outside of the self yet inside its Umwelt and still not reducible to purely objective being. Again mark the difference from a *res cogitans*: the rationality of the rational animal may be abstractly considered as closed unto itself, but experientially it is bound up with and inseparable from otherness; and this same rationality, as the capacity for being reasonable, appears against the horizon of otherness not abstractly and closed off but rather as — precisely — the ability to grasp the reason of things presented within objectivity. Hence Petrilli can say that,[14] "given the risks inherent in social reproduction today for semiosis and for life, human beings must at their very earliest transform themselves from rational animals into reasonable animals" in the semiotic sense, animals able to deal with otherness on the basis of a grasp of the "reasons of things", a grasp which cannot be come by in isolation, but requires experience as a web of relations which sustains both self and other as ground for the possibility of flourishing. "Under the hardened crust of its identity", Petrilli says:[15]

> the subject rediscovers its fear for the other, for the other's safety through love. Such fear renders the subject incessantly rest-

---

[13] Ibid. 112, emphasis shifted from "reason" to "of things".

[14] Ibid.

[15] Ibid.

less and preoccupied for the other. Love, reasonableness, creativity are all grounded in the logic of otherness and dialogism.

6. Passing the Limits of Modern Thought

In the *res cogitans*, the intermediate modern stage of development of the human species, the human being became aware of its rationality especially as something separating it from the rest of nature. In the semiotic animal, the modern experiment has passed its limits with the realization that rationality is by itself not yet reasonableness, for "reasonableness is the capacity to respond to the attraction exerted upon the self by the other",[16] not the isolation of the self from the other. Wojtyła has described this overcoming of the modern interlude in just such terms of the necessity and irreducibility of experience to the individual:[17]

> While explaining thus [i.e., metaphysically] the reality of the human being, there remains each time ... the respective 'experience lived through' [*Erlebnis*] as an aspect not directly included in this metaphysical explanation or reduction, since it is an irreducible element. From the point of view of the metaphysical structure of being and action, and therefore from the point of view of the dynamics of man when he is conceived metaphysically, dealing with this element may seem unnecessary. We may acquire a sufficient understanding of the human being, of its action and of what occurs within, also without it. For many centuries, on such an understanding the whole edifice of anthropology and ethics was being constructed. But as the need of understanding the human being as an only and unique person grows, and especially as the need of understanding the personal subjectivity of man in the whole dynamics of action and occurrence proper to him keeps growing, the category of 'experience lived through' gathers meaning, and, what is more, a key meaning. ... the chief aim of this is to show the person as a subject living

---

[16] Ibid., 113.
[17] Karol Wojtyła 1978: 110.

through one's own deeds and experiences, and thanks to all this, one's own subjectivity. When this demand is made upon the interpretation of 'the acting human being', the category of 'experience lived through' must find its place in anthropology and ethics and, what is more, must to a certain degree take its place in the center of respective interpretations.

So the "reasonable animal", who begins to try to take into account the "reasons of things" (for example, in becoming aware of the environmental impact of greenhouse gases, etc.), marks the late modern transition from the *res cogitans* to the semiotic animal. But it may be said that the transition from *res cogitans* to semiotic animal in another way, and more fundamentally, is not gradual. This transition marks a frontier, the frontier of postmodernity. Not until it is realized that "the keystone of the life of the mind is the sign",[18] and the consequences of this realization begin to surge into consciousness, do we have the right to speak of the semiotic animal; for a semiotic animal, as mentioned above, is an animal that lives with the awareness of the action of signs as more fundamental to the constitution of human experience than are either objects or things.

The point first, or at least best so far, made by Petrilli and Ponzio[19] — that the human being, as the only semiotic animal on earth, *eo ipso* assumes the burden, like it or not, of a unique responsibility — is the point of further transition, as it were, *from* semiotic animal merely becoming aware of the being and action proper to signs *to* that same animal coming to see itself *semioethically*, that is to say, as *accepting responsibility* inevitably for that being and action *as bearing on the welfare of the human race inseparable from the whole biosphere* from which the race of semiotic animals is inseparable. Semiotics goes not only global, but cosmic, as it were, as the semiotic animal expands also into space beyond planet earth as part of its *Lebenswelt*. Petrilli and Ponzio describe this further awareness as a "third dimension" concerned with "the ends toward

---

[18] Maritain 1957: 3.
[19] Petrilli and Ponzio 2003.

which we strive and wish to reach", an awareness "with respect to semiosis over the whole planet"; and I say, if the conquest of space seriously materializes, even beyond our planet.

7. The Trajectory to Postmodernity

It is remarkable to observe the development semiotics has undergone as we move into the 21st century. From an early florescence in the 20th century as "semiology" and "structuralism" which knew not the difference between idealism and realism and in practice embraced the former as best providing a field of play for analysts of signs (an ultramodern position mistaken by many for a "postmodernism"[20]), semiotics little by little gained its footing as the doctrine of signs "at the intersection of nature and culture", as Sebeok best put it, far from mired down on the idealist side of the idealism/realism debate but rather the first intellectual tradition to emerge beyond the very terms of that debate as able to take into account, while transcending, the focus of both camps.

The crucial discovery, as I have said, lay in the realization that the being of signs does not consist in anything sense-perceptible as such but wholly in the transcending, the 'suprasubjective', relation as such tying together triadically what is sense-perceptible so as to

---

[20] Sebeok 1996: 53: "The most unfortunate development in semiotics has been a movement which you might call postmodernism ... an abortion started in Paris, and undergoing various forms and transmutations involving such individuals ... as Roland Barthes, Jacques Lacan, Foucault, and most destructively in my opinion Derrida. I think these people ... and not only my friend Julia Kristeva did a great disservice to semiotics by pretending that they were doing semiotics, where in fact they were doing, let me say, antisemiotics. This misled a great many people, particularly in the humanities ... such people as English department teachers, French department teachers, comparative literature types ... these people did such ridiculous things that the serious thinkers, like the good philosophers, the scientists, physicists, biologists, just laughed and threw up their hands .... This did a great disservice to North American and European university life, to a lesser extent in Asia. ... I think ... this [falsely so-called] postmodern stuff is now, in my opinion, and thank God, disappearing." These rather scathing remarks by Sebeok apply to an *ultramodernism* rather than to anything truly *post*modern, as I have set forth at length in Deely 2001: Chap. 16.

form a meaningful world of objects.[21] The ancients debated the distinction between intellect and sense in terms of the human being's ability to grasp being beyond the sensible. The medievals did the same. The moderns thought rather in terms of perception and understanding and tended to reduce the latter to the field of the former. Semiotics showed that signs do not fall strictly among the things objectified by perceptions of sense but act prior to that perception to enable it to reconstruct the physical environment along objective lines that are meaningful to the species, into an Umwelt, as is now commonly said. To this Umwelt the semiotic animal brings a unique realization, the realization that, even as things presuppose objects in order to be discovered and known within them, so objects presuppose the action of signs in order to be constructed and formed into a world meaningful differently for each variety and species of living thing.

But, in discovering the imperceptible being of signs perceptibly acting in weaving the relations of meaning that constitute the world as an Umwelt, or, rather, series of Umwelts — objective worlds species-specific to each type of animal — the semiotic animal also discovers how nature enters into the objective order of what is signified, the Umwelt, and plays its irreducible and indispensable role in contributing to objectivity mind-independent relations alongside and interwoven with the mind-dependent ones which provenate from the unique self-identity maintained over and above, as a "surplus" respecting, biological or even cultural individuality. Petrilli[22] cites Peirce's British interlocutor Lady Welby as observing that "we have all entered the world precisely to be dissatisfied with it." This dissatisfaction has at its root the difference between the world of objects which only incompletely incorporates the environment of things, and the action and interaction of those things themselves which is essential to the well-being of Umwelts regardless of whether it is known (objectified) or not.

---

[21] See Deely 2001a. Also YouTube <http://www.youtube.com/view_play_list?p=E9651802BCDC14BF> (= "semiotic sign", in five videos).

[22] Petrilli 2003: 113.

What the semiotic animal alone among the animals is in a position ontologically to take into account is precisely this *shifting boundary* between what is and what we are aware of as being (a boundary that modern philosophy after Kant disastrously attempted to render fixed once and for all, with the distinction between Ding-an-sich and Noumenon as exhaustively embracing the "unknowable"[23]), a boundary sustained in its entire extent by the action of signs.

8. Semioethics within Semiotics

So it seems to me that semioethics cannot be conceived as a moving beyond semiotics, but rather (and only) as an inevitable development of semiotics from within, one necessary to the health of the biosphere insofar as humans are involved with it; for semio-ethics is nothing more nor less than an *ethics stringently derived from semiosis* itself — that is, an ethics developed within anthroposemio-sis become conscious (through metasemiosis) of human respon-sibility seen as an outgrowth of nature itself binding our species to nature in a new way, yes, but not at all as something setting the human species apart from nature as a whole respecting which we can afford to be indifferent and to dominate as we please.[24] Simple

---

[23] On this crucial Kantian distinction, often conflated, see Deely 2001b: in Chapter 13, pp. 553–572, esp. 558–559; and the discussion above in Chapter 2, p. 5, and Chapter 7, p. 42 text and note 9.

[24] The semioethic view is similar to that of Levinas 1967: 225: "Nous appelons éthique une relation entre des termes où l'un et l'autre ne sont unis ni par une synthèse de l'entendement ni par la relation de sujet à objet et où cependant l'un pèse ou importe ou est signifiant à l'autre, où ils sont liés par une intrigue que le savoir ne saurait ni épuiser ni démêler" — "We call ethical a relationship between terms such as are united neither by a synthesis of the understanding nor by a re-lationship between subject and object, and yet where the one weighs or concerns or is meaningful to the other, where they are bound by a plot which knowing can neither exhaust nor unravel". Yet it is not a question of any simple priority of "ethics" overall, for without the awareness distinctive of human understanding the question of *any* ethics cannot even arise.

On Levinas within semiotics, therefore, see Deely 2009f: 251–252n32. It is the old Scholastic question of the comparative priority of "intellect" and "will" in context anew. Precisely and only because human understanding has access to Firstness by reason of its singular grasp of "being" (*ens primum cognitum*) prior to

domination, we come to realize, imperils not only the life forms dominated but, redundantly, our own life form as itself part of the semiosphere linking all of life. The question goes back to an old contrast first thematized by Aristotle: the difference between speculative and practical knowledge. It is true that Aristotle in a certain sense misconceived this contrast, by casting it in purely objective rather than semiotic terms, and conceiving it within the framework of a conception, legitimate in its time (though for all that legitimacy thoroughly mistaken), of a universe unchanging in its specific structures. Thus Aristotle conceived of speculative knowledge as concerned with objects of awareness respecting which human thought and action can have no impact, in contrast with practical thought concerned with objects that would not be as they were it not precisely for human beliefs and actions — such objective realities as the state, the family, and the behavior of individuals as better or worse, right or wrong.

Aquinas in the medieval interval did a little better, by noting that practical thought to be effective depends upon and must take its measure from speculative understanding, whence, as speculative understanding grows, *so does the province of practical thought* as able to extend a human impact upon the surrounding environment of physical being. Aquinas, to be sure, did not envision global warming, or even the evolution of species, but he did envision the reason that human beings can in principle do something about climate destabilization and intervene in the matter of the biological development of life forms. In this Aquinas anticipated Francis Bacon with his idea for a *Novum Organum*, such as science has placed in our hands. But Aquinas differed not a whit from Aristotle in conceiving this distinction between speculative and practical in primarily objective terms. The discovery that objects presuppose signs still lay

---

(because transcending) recognition of difference between what in objectivity is mind-dependent and what mind-independent imposed by Secondness can it be said (Petrilli 2009: 1370) that "the gaze of semioethics transcends the totality, a given being, a defined entity within a totality and accounts for infinite semiosis, desire of the other, unending movement toward the infinite".

three-hundred-fifty years ahead, in the *Tractatus de Signis* of John
Poinsot, Aquinas' most brilliant postmortem pupil among the Latins, as Maritain best noted.[25]

It remains that the recognition of a distinctive sphere of practical
thought, that is to say, the realm of what human beings by their beliefs
and actions can do something about, can make otherwise than they
found it initially, was the original province and meaning of "ethics"
and "ethical knowledge". Yet no less important remains the recognition that such knowledge as specifically human is derivative from
and dependent for its effective exercise upon speculative knowledge
of the way things are according to their intrinsic physical constitution as interacting individuals. "The speculative understanding or
intellect", as Aquinas put it,[26] "becomes practical by extension." Animals other than humans know only objects and objects which are
sign-vehicles, and care not a whit for any difference between objects
and things, because they have no way of making such a difference
into a factor of awareness in their dealings with the world. Human
animals become aware of a difference between objects which are
and are not in any given context sign-vehicles, and they even mistake the sign-vehicles for signs, and (as Heidegger well complained)
objects *tout court* for things.

But a new kind of animal is born, the semiotic animal, as the
human animals become aware not only of the difference between
objects and things, but more profoundly of the difference between
sign-vehicles and signs in their proper being as triadic relations presupposed to the world of objects and essential to the well-being of
animals within a physical environment which, at any given time (and
for any given species of animal), is only partially and aspectually objectified, even in essential matters bearing on the continuance in
being of the species. As the rational animal assumed its burden of
practical awareness in terms of recognizing the need for that body of
thought traditionally called "ethics", as the *res cogitans* indulged itself

---

[25] Cf. Maritain 1953: esp. vi.

[26] Aquinas 1266: *Summa theologiae* I, Ques. 79, Art. 11, *sed contra*.

for centuries in solipsistic reveries of idle speculation while the world around it continued on its semiosic path of evolution,[27] so the rational animal toward the end of modern times woke up to the need to become more *reasonable* in contrast to abstract "rationality".The way was thus prepared for the semiotic animal, and for semioethics as naming the extension of semiotic awareness to that *unfixed* boundary of intersection between nature and culture where the semiotic animal can, by taking account of the reasons of things, make a difference for the better (or the worse!), a difference upon which, it becomes increasingly clear, not only the semiotic animal as one among the biological lifeforms but the biosphere itself and the whole of Gaia (in Lovelock's sense) may ultimately depend for continuance.

9. A New Humanism

Petrilli and Ponzio see the situation of the semiotic animal as the birth of "a new form of humanism", a "humanism of alterity" contrasting with the traditional "humanisms of identity" by not leaving out the *rights of the other* and the importance of the other *independent of its status as human* but rather reconceptualizing the whole matter of interdependency as one "where the rights of the other are the first to be recognized", because these rights include also my own as also an "other" respecting all that surrounds me.

I think the recognition that the boundaries of semiotic reality are never fixed and always shifting is the key realization[28] for this

---

[27] Precisely what modern philosophy ruled out, semiotics provides (Petrilli 2003: 108):"the critical distancing necessary for an interpretation of contemporaneity that is not imprisoned within the limits of contemporaneity itself."

[28] Petrilli 2003: 110: "If semiotics is to meet its commitment to the 'health of semiosis' and to cultivate its capacity to understand the entire semiosic universe, it must continuously refine its auditory and critical functions, that is, its capacity for listening and critique. And to accomplish such tasks we believe that the trichotomy that distinguishes between (1) cognitive semiotics, (2) global semiotics, and (3) semioethics is no less than decisive, not only in theoretical terms, but also for reasons of a therapeutic order." I am not so sure of this trichotomy, but I am sure that, within anthroposemiotics, semioethics "concerns the ends towards which we strive and wish to reach."

new, this postmodern, humanism, wherein traditional objective
"ethics" is transformed as "semioethics" by the discovery that human knowledge in the whole of its extent — speculative no less
than practical[29] — depends upon the action of signs, an action
that is presupposed to every "world of objects", every Umwelt
around the whole planet (or elsewhere in this universe, as the case
may be). Things may pre-exist us in various ways, but only as they
are translated into objects can we intelligently deal with them.
And since there is (and can be) no single path for this translation, it is especially the procedures of abductive and retroductive
logic on which we above all depend for the translation, and the
'translation' can only be understood "in the broadest sense possible, that is to say, beyond the limits of interlingual translation,
translation as interpretation and verification of verbal and nonverbal signs alike."[30]

Petrilli sees the situation as a "Third Copernican Revolution",
Kant having been the second,[31] now overthrown by the discovery of an action of signs which allows no fixed boundary either
between sensory intuition and things-in-themselves or between
concepts and noumena. But I think it is not a matter of the point
where "global semiotics" and "semioethics intersect." Not at all.
For semiotics and semioethics are not independent developments,
but reciprocal aspects of a single development: the evolution of
human understanding. Semioethics is nothing more than the ma-
turing consciousness of the semiotic animal become aware as self-
evident of the truth, as Sebeok put it,[32] that "each and every man,
woman, and child superintends over a partially shared pool of signs
in which that same monadic being is immersed and must navigate
for survival throughout its singular life"; for that is the context that

---

[29] See "Semiotica utramque comprehendit" ("Semiotics embraces both"), in Deely 2003: 100–112.

[30] Petrilli 2003: 113.

[31] But cf. Deely 2001: 565–572.

[32] Sebeok 2001: ix. On this notion of "self-evident", recall note 29 of Chapter 7 from p. 50 above.

postmodernity realizes as the sphere within which *bonum faciendum est*, the ethical goal is to be realized.

10. In Sum

Semioethics, in short, is nothing more nor less than the question of what are we going to do about, how are we going to handle, the fact that human beings are not merely "rational animals", still less *res cogitantes*, but, in the fulness of their species-specifically unique being, semiotic animals, each and every one, an animal to and for whom *nil semiosica alienum me cogitabile est*. It is a unique responsibility, alright, springing from the awareness of semiosis as embracing the whole planet, of times past, present, and to come, and of our impact upon it as the only semiotic animals within the Gaia.

References, Historically Layered

AQUINAS, Thomas (1224/5–1274).
   i.1252–1273. *S. Thomae Aquinatis Opera Omnia ut sunt in indice thomis-tico*, ed. Roberto Busa (Stuttgart-Bad Cannstatt: Frommann-Holzboog, 1980), in septem volumina.
   c.1254/6. *In quattuor libros sententiarum Petri Lombardi*, in Busa ed. vol. 1.
   c.1266/73. *Summa theologiae*, in Busa ed. vol. 2, 184–926.
   c.1268/72. *In duodecim libros metaphysicorum Aristotelis expositio*, in Busa ed. vol. 4, 390–507.

ARBIB, Michael A.
   1971. "How We Know Universals: Retrospect and Prospect", *Mathematical Biosciences* 11, 95–107.

ARISTOTLE (384–322BC).
   c.348–330BC. *Metaphysics*, in Vol. 2, pp. 1552–1728, of *Aristotle: The Complete Works*, being the Revised Oxford Translation of W. D. Ross's 1928–1952 edition titled *The Complete Works of Aristotle*, the revision having been done under the editorship of Jonathan Barnes (Princeton, NJ: Princeton University Press, 1984); available in electronic form from Intelex Corp. (Charlottesville, Virginia).
   i.348–334BC. *Politics*, trans. Benjamin Jowett, in *The Basic Works of Aristotle*, ed. Richard McKeon (New York: Basic Books, 1941), pp. 1113–1316. The 19th and 20th century English translators of Aristotle have tended to render the term λογον minimalistically as "speech". But this is to confuse — as Sebeok first pointed out within semiotics (1984 and after) — linguistic communication, which is an exaptation, with language itself, the adaptation of the human Innenwelt species-specific thereto as a modeling system that is biologically underdetermined and creative of the prior possibility of linguistic

communication as a species-specifically human communicative modality.

BAER, Eugen.
1977.   "Things Are Stories: A Manifesto for a Reflexive Semiotics", *Semiotica* 25.3–24, 293/205.
1982.   "The Medical Symptom", *The American Journal of Semiotics* 1.3, 17–34; corrected and reprinted in Deely, Williams, and Kruse 1986: 140–152.
1988.   *Medical Semiotics: The State of the Art* (=Sources in Semiotics VII; Lanham, MD: University Press of America).
1992.   "Via Semiotica", *Semiotica* 92.3–24, 351/357.

BEUCHOT, Mauricio.
1980.   "La doctrina tomista clásica sobre el signo: Domingo de Soto, Francisco de Araújo y Juan de Santo Tomás", *Critica* XII.36 (México, diciembre), 39–60.
1983.   "Los terminos y las categorías sintactico-semanticas en la lógica post-medieval", *Diánoia* 29, 175–196.
1986.   "Signo y Lenguaje en San Augustín", *Dianoia* (anuario de filosofia), 32, 13–26.
1987.   *Metafísica: La Ontología Aristotélico-Tomista de Francisco de Araújo* (México City: Universidad Nacional Autónoma de México).
1991.   "El realismo cognoscitivo en Santo Tomás de Aquino. Sus condiciones metafísicas", *Diánoia* 37, 49–60.
1993.   "La percepción sensible en Santo Tomás de Aquino", in *Percepción: Colores*, ed. Laura Benítez and José A. Robles (= La Filosofía y Sus Problemas; México City: Universidad Nacional Autónoma, Instituto de Investigaciones Filosóficas), 11–29.
1993a. "El argumento 'ontológico' de San Anselmo", *Medievalia* 15 (diciembre), 24–31.
1994.   "Intentionality in John Poinsot", in *American Catholic Philosophical Quarterly* 68.3 (Summer), 279–296.
1995.   *Escolastica Ibérica Post-Medieval- Algunas Teorías del Signo*, selección de textos, introducción y traducción (Maracaibo y Caracas, Venezuela: Universidad del Zulia y Universidad Católica Andrés).
1998.   "Bañez, Domingo (1528–1604)", entry in the *Routledge Encyclopedia of Philosophy*, ed. in 10 volumes by Edward Craig (London: Routledge, 1998), Vol. 1, pp. 647–649.

BEUCHOT, Mauricio, Editor and Translator.

1995.   *Algunas Teorías del Signo en la Escolastica Iberica Post-Medieval*, selección de textos, introducción y traducción (Maracaibo y Caracas, Venezuela: Universidad del Zulia y Universidad Católica Andrés).

BEUCHOT, Mauricio, and John DEELY.

1995.   "Common Sources for the Semiotic of Charles Peirce and John Poinsot", *Review of Metaphysics* XLVIII.3 (March 1995), 539–566.

BREZIK, Victor B. (2 May 1913–2009 June 16), Editor.

1981.   *One Hundred Years of Thomism: Aeterni Patris and Afterwards. A Symposium [held 4–5 October 1979]* (Houston, TX: University of St. Thomas Center for Thomistic Studies).

CAJETAN, Thomas de Vio Cajetan (20 February 1469–1534 August 9).

1507.   *Commentaria in summam theologicam. Prima pars*, reprinted in the Leonine edition of the *Sancti Thomae Aquinatis Doctoris Angelici Opera Omnia*, vols. 4 and 5 (Rome, 1888–1889).

CASSIRER, Ernst (28 July 1874–1945 April 13).

1944.   *An Essay on Man: An introduction to a Philosophy of Human Culture* (New Haven: Yale University Press).

COBLEY, Paul, Editor.

2009.   *Realism for the 21st Century: A John Deely Reader* (Scranton, PA: University of Scranton Press).

COLAPIETRO, Vincent (1950–), and Thomas OLSHEWSKY (1934–), Editors.

1996.   *Peirce's Doctrine of Signs* (Berlin: Mouton de Gruyter).

CONIMBRICENSES.

1607.   "De Signis", being Chapter 1 of their commentary on Aristotle's *De Interpretatione*, in *Commentarii Collegii Conimbricensis et Societatis Jesu. In Universam Dialecticam Aristotelis Stagiritae. Secunda Pars* (Lyons: Sumptibus Horatii Cardon, 1607), pp. 4–67. An earlier edition minus the Greek text of Aristotle was published at Coimbra itself in 1606. See Doyle ed. 2001 for an English translation in a bilingual critical edition of this work.

COSERIU, Eugenio.
  1967.   "L'arbitraire du signe: zur Spätgeschichte eines aristotelischen Beggriffes", Archiv für *das Studium der Neueren sprachen und Literaturen* 204, 81–112.

COTTINGHAM, John (1943–), Robert STOOTHOFF, and Dugald MURDOCH
  (1944–), Translators.
  1985.   *The Philosophical Writings of Descartes* (Cambridge, England: Cambridge University Press), 2 vols.

DEACON, Terrence.
  1997.   *The Symbolic Species: the Co-Evolution of Language and the Brain* (New York: W. W. Norton & Company).

DEELY, John.
  1971.   "Animal Intelligence and Concept-Formation", *The Thomist* XXXV.1 (January), 43–93.
  1976.   "The Doctrine of Signs: Taking Form at Last", *Semiotica* 18:2, 171–193. Essay review of Umberto Eco, *A Theory of Semiotics*, English trans. by David Osmond-Smith (Bloomington: Indiana University Press) of *Trattato di semiotica generale* (Milan: Bompiani, 1975).
  1977.   "'Semiotic' as the Doctrine of Signs", *Ars Semeiotica* 1/3, 41–68.
  1978.   "What's in a Name?", *Semiotica* 22.1–2, 151–181. Essay review of Thomas A. Sebeok, *Contributions to the Doctrine of Signs* (Bloomington, IN, and Lisse, Netherlands: Publication of the Research Center for Language and Semiotic Studies of Indiana University, together with The Peter De Ridder Press). Reprinted with an extended Prefatory Essay by Brooke Williams Deely, "Challenging Signs at the Crossroads", evaluating the book in light of major reviews (=Sources in Semiotics IV; Lanham, MD: University Press of America, 1985).
  1980.   "The Nonverbal Inlay in Linguistic Communication", in Rauch and Carr 1980: 201–217.
  1982.   *Introducing Semiotic: Its History and Doctrine* (Bloomington, IN: Indiana University Press).
  1982a. "On the Notion 'Doctrine of Signs'", Appendix I in Deely 1982: 127–130.

1982b. "On the Notion of Phytosemiotics", in *Semiotics 1982*, ed. John Deely and Jonathan Evans (Lanham, MD: University Press of America, 1987), 541–554; reprinted with minor revision in Deely, Williams, and Kruse, eds. 1986: 96–103.

1985. "Editorial AfterWord" and critical apparatus to *Tractatus de Signis: The Semiotic of John Poinsot* (Berkeley: University of California Press), 391–514; electronic version hypertext-linked (Charlottesville, VA: Intelex Corp.; see entry under Poinsot 1632a below).

1985a. "Semiotic and the Liberal Arts", *The New Scholasticism* LIX.3 (Summer), 296–322. The "second epsilon" mentioned in this work is a blunder, for the "first epsilon" in the Greek "semeiotic" is not an epsilon but an eta, thus: Σημειωτική.

1986. "Semiotic in the Thought of Jacques Maritain", *Recherche Sémiotique/ Semiotic Inquiry* 6.2, 1–30.

1986a. "A Context for Narrative Universals. Semiology as a *Pars Semeiotica*", *The American Journal of Semiotics* 4.3–4 (1986), 53–68.

1986b. "Doctrine", terminological entry for the *Encyclopedic Dictionary of Semiotics*, ed. Thomas A. Sebeok et al. (Berlin: Mouton de Gruyter), Tome I, p. 214.

1988. "The Semiotic of John Poinsot: Yesterday and Tomorrow", *Semiotica* 69.1/2 (April, 1988), 31–127.

1990. *Basics of Semiotics* (Bloomington, IN: Indiana University Press).

1991. "Semiotics and Biosemiotics: Are Sign-Science and Life-Science Coextensive?", in *Biosemiotics. The Semiotic Web 1991*, ed. Thomas Sebeok and Jean Umiker-Sebeok (Berlin: Mouton de Gruyter, 1992), 45–75.

1992. "Philosophy and Experience", *American Catholic Philosophical Quarterly* LXVI.4 (Winter), 299–319.

1993. "Semiotics in the United States and Beyond", Special Issue guest-ed. John Deely and Susan Petrilli, *Semiotica* 97–3/4.

1993a. "How Does Semiosis Effect Renvoi?", the Thomas A. Sebeok Fellowship Inaugural Address delivered at the 18th Annual Meeting of the Semiotic Society of America, October 22, 1993, St. Louis, MO; published in *The American Journal of Semiotics* 11.1–2 (1994), 11–61. Reprinted in Deely 1994a: 201–244.

1994.   *New Beginnings: Early Modern Philosophy and Postmodern Thought* (Toronto, Canada: University of Toronto Press).

1994a.   *The Human Use of Signs, or Elements of Anthroposemiosis* (Lanham, MD: Rowman & Littlefield).

1995.   "The Intersemiosis of Perception and Understanding", paper presented in Oporto, Portugal, and immediately commissioned for publication by Richard Lanigan, in the Oporto audience, as editor of *The American Journal of Semiotics*. Actual publication was in TAJS 20.1–4 (2004), 211–253.

1995a.   "Ferdinand de Saussure and Semiotics", in *Ensaios em Homagem a Thomas A. Sebeok*, quadruple Special Issue of *Cruzeiro Semiótico*, ed. Norma Tasca (Porto, Portugal: Fundação Eng. António de Almeida), 75–85. Revised text appears under same title in *Semiotics 1995*, ed. C. W. Spinks and John Deely (New York: Peter Lang, 1996), 71–83.

1997.   "The Seven Deadly Sins and the Catholic Church", *Semiotica* 117–2/4 (1997), 67–71.

1998.   "Augustine of Hippo", entry in Paul Bouissac, ed., *Encyclopedia of Semiotics* (New York: Oxford University Press), 51–53.

1998a.   "Poinsot, Joannes", entry in Paul Bouissac, ed., *Encyclopedia of Semiotics* (New York: Oxford University Press), 498–500.

1998b.   "Medieval Semiotics", entry in Paul Bouissac, ed., *Encyclopedia of Semiotics* (New York: Oxford University Press), 399–404.

1999.   *The Red Book* and *The Green Book*, at <http://www.helsinki.fi/science/commens/papers.html>.

2000.   "The Latin Foundations for Semiotic Consciousness: Augustine (5th cent. AD) to Poinsot (17th cent. AD)", *Recherches Sémiotique/Semiotic Inquiry* 20.1–2–3, 11–32; revised version of presentation made 11 October to "Das Europäische Erbe der Smiotik" conference held at the Technical University of Dresden 18–21 February 1999.

2001.   *Four Ages of Understanding: The First Postmodern History of Philosophy from Ancient Times to the Turn of the 21st Century* (Toronto, Canada: University of Toronto Press).

2001a.   "Physiosemiosis in the Semiotic Spiral: A Play of Musement", *Sign Systems Studies* 29.1, 27–46.

2001b.   "Umwelt", *Semiotica* 134–1/4, 125–135.

2001c. "A Sign is *What?*", *Sign Systems Studies* 29.2 (2001), 705–743; Presidential Address to the Semiotic Society of America's 26th Annual Meeting held at Victoria College of the University of Toronto, Canada, October 19, 2001. Reprinted as "Dialogue between a 'Semiotist' and a 'Realist'" in *The Impact on Philosophy of Semiotics. The Quasi-Error of the External World, with a Dialogue between a 'Semiotist' and a 'Realist'* (South Bend, IN: St. Augustine's Press, 2003), 157–208; and more fully formatted for stage presentation in "Dramatic Reading in Three Voices: 'A Sign Is *What?*'," *The American Journal of Semiotics* 20.1–4 (2004), 1–66 (= 2001b reformatted with numbered lines for presentation as a three-voice dramatic reading). Partially presented live at <http://www.youtube.com/view_play_list?p=E9651802BCDC14BF>.

2002. *What Distinguishes Human Understanding?* (South Bend, IN: St. Augustine's Press).

2003. *The Impact on Philosophy of Semiotics: The Quasi-Error of the External World, with a Dialogue between a 'Semiotist' and a 'Realist'* (South Bend, IN: St. Augustine's Press).

2003a. "The semiotic animal" (first systematic draft), in Petrilli and Calefato eds., *Logica, dialogica, ideologica. I segni tra funzionalita ed eccedenza* (= itinerari filosofici; Milan: Mimesis, 2003), 201–219; also in *The Second Renaissance* (Milan: Spirali).

2003b. "The semiotic animal" (humanist version), presented in the Monday, 22 September, 2003 'Metaphysical Session', of the International Congress "Christian Humanism in the Third Millennium", Rome, 21–25 September 2003; web version posted on Congress site <http://e-aquinas.net/pdf/deely.pdf.>; hardcopy Congress proceedings in preparation.

2003c. "The Semiotic Animal" (definitional version), in *Semiotics 2003*, ed. Rodney Williamson, Leonard Sbrocchi, and John Deely (Ottawa, Canada: Legas). Presented as a colloquium at the Center for Thomistic Studies of the University of St. Thomas, Houston, 23 October 2003.

2003d. "The Word 'Semiotics': Formation and Origins", *Semiotica* 146–1/4, 1–49.

2003e. "If the heart can be replaced, why not the soul?", presented at the April 9 "Culture versus Technology" conference at the

Catholic University of Lublin, Poland; forthcoming in the Proceedings.

2004.   *Why Semiotics?* (Ottawa: Legas).

2004a.   "Why the Semiotic Animal Needs to Develop a Semio-ethics", presented Sunday, July 11, as part of Round Table 008 "Issues in Socio-Semiotics" of the 8th IASS Congress, Lyon, France, 7–12 July 2004, at Université Lumière Lyon 2, sponsored by the International Rossi-Landi Network (FRIN); now published as paper #72 in *Semiotics 2008*, ed. John Deely and Leonard Sbrocchi (Ottawa: Legas, 2009), pp. 716–729.

2004b.   "From Semiotic Animal to Semioethical Animal and Back", in *Macht der Zeichen, Zeichen der Macht / Signs of Power, Power of Signs* (Festschrift für Jeff Bernard; =Trans-Studien zur Ve-raenderung der Welt 3), ed. Gloria Witthalm and Josef Wall-mannsberger (Wien: Lit.Verlag), 120–136.

2004c.   "The Semiosis of Angels", *The Thomist* 68.2 (April 2004), 205–258.

2004d.   "Semiotics and Jakob von Uexküll's Concept of Umwelt", presented 10 January 2004 at the 9–10 January 2004 Inter-national Symposium "Zeichen und der Bauplan des Leb-ens — Uexkülls Bedeutung heute" opening the Jakob von Uexküll-Archiv at the University of Hamburg; text forth-coming in *Sign System Studies* (Tartu University, Estonia).

2004e.   "Iberian Fingerprints on the Doctrine of Signs", *The Ameri-can Journal of Semiotics* 20.1–4, 93–156.

2004f.   "The Thomistic Import of the Neo-Kantian Concept of Umwelt in Jakob von Uexküll", *Angelicum* 81.4, 711–732.

2005a.   *Purely Objective Reality* (preliminary essay to the complete work, 2009a below; Southeast European Center for Semi-otic Studies 2005 Seminar Series Publication; Sofia, Bulgaria: New Bulgarian University).

2005b.   *Thomas Albert Sebeok and Semiotics* (Southeast European Center for Semiotic Studies 2005 Seminar Series Publica-tion; Sofia, Bulgaria: New Bulgarian University).

2005c.   "Defining the Semiotic Animal: How the postmodern under-standing of human being supersedes the modern definition 'res cogitans'," in Deely, Petrilli, and Ponzio 2005: 145–186.

2005d. "Defining the Semiotic Animal: A Postmodern Definition of Human Being Superseding the Modern Definition 'Res Cogitans'," *American Catholic Philosophical Quarterly* 79.3 (Summer 2005), 461–481. Abbreviated and revised version of 2005.

2005e. *Defining the Semiotic Animal* (Sofia, Bulgaria: New Bulgarian University 2005 Seminar Series Publication, Southeast European Center for Semiotic Studies).

2005f. "The Semiotic Foundations of the Human Sciences from Augustine to Peirce", *Recherche Sémiotique/Semiotic Inquiry* 22.1–2–3 (2003), 3–29. Presented on Friday, 26 March, at the International Congress "Semiotics and the Humanities" jointly organized by Chinese Academy of Social Sciences and International Association for Semiotic Studies Beijing, China 25–29 March 2004.

2006. "Semiotics, History of", in *Encyclopedia of Language and Linguistics, Second Edition* (London: Elsevier), Vol. 11, 216–229.

2006a. "On 'Semiotics' as Naming the Doctrine of Signs", *Semiotica* 158.1/4 (2006), 1–33.

2006b. "The literal, the metaphorical, and the price of semiotics: an essay on philosophy of language and the doctrine of signs", *Semiotica* 161–1/4 (2006), 9–74.

2006c. "Augustine, Saint, Theory of the Sign", in *Encyclopedia of Language and Linguistics, Second Edition*, Keith Brown Editor-in-Chief (London: Elsevier), Vol. 1, 574–577.

2007. *Intentionality and Semiotics: A Story of Mutual Fecundation* (Scranton, PA: University of Scranton Press).

2008. "Evolution, Semiosis, and Ethics: Rethinking the Context of Natural Law", in *Contemporary Perspectives on Natural Law*, ed. Ana Marta González (Aldershot, England: Ashgate, 2008), 413–442.

2008a. "From Semiosis to Semioethics: The Full Vista of the Action of Signs", *Sign System Studies* 36.2, 437–421. This essay in a slightly revised and expanded form, becomes Chapter 12 of 2009b: 233–275 (see esp. Section 4.3.2., pp. 262–263).

2008b. *Descartes & Poinsot: The Crossroad of Signs and Ideas* (Scranton, PA: University of Scranton Press).

2009. *Augustine & Poinsot: The Protosemiotic Development* (Scranton, PA: Scranton University Press).

2009a.   *Purely Objective Reality* (Berlin: Mouton de Gruyter).

2009b.   *Basics of Semiotics*, expanded 5th edition (Tartu, Estonia: Tartu University Press).

2009c.   *Realism for the 21st Century. A John Deely Reader*, ed. Paul Cobley (Scranton, PA: Scranton University Press).

2009d.   "Aristotle's Triangle and the Triadic Sign", Prologue to *Semiotics 2008* (Proceedings of the 33rd Annual SSA Meeting held in Houston, Texas, October 16–19, 2008; Toronto, Canada: Legas), xlix–xc.

2009e.   "Pars Pro Toto from Culture to Nature" (TAJS editorial overview of semiotics as a postmodern development, with particular focus on biosemiotics), *The American Journal of Semiotics* 25.1–2 (2009), 167–192.

2009f.   *Basics of Semiotics*, expanded 5th edition (Tartu Semiotics Library 4.2; Tartu, Estonia: Tartu University Press).

2009g.   "Postmodernity and the Unmasking of Objectivity", plenary lecture presented 7 June 2009 to the International Semiotics Institute (ISI) 2009 June 5–9 Summer School for Semiotic Studies in Imatra, Finland; printed by ISI in booklet for the occasion.

2010.   "The Unmasking of Objectivity", in *History, Being, and Singularity: A Festscrift in Honor of Kenneth Schmitz*, ed. Michael Baur and Robert E. Wood (Washington, D.C.: The Catholic Unviersity of America Press).

DEELY, John, Susan PETRILLI, and Augusto PONZIO.

2005.   *The Semiotic Animal* (Ottawa, Canada: Legas Publishing).

DEELY, John N., Brooke WILLIAMS, and Felicia E. KRUSE, editors.

1986.   *Frontiers in Semiotics* (Bloomington: Indiana University Press). Preface titled "Pars Pro Toto", pp. viii–xvii; "Description of Contributions", pp. xviii–xxii.

DESCARTES, René (31 March 1596–1650 February 11).

1628.   *Rules for the Direction of the Mind*, trans. Dugald Murdoch in Cottingham, Stoothoff, and Murdoch trans. 1985: I, 9–78.

1637.   *Discourse on the Method of Rightly Conducting One's Reason and Seeking Truth in the Sciences*, trans. Robert Stoothoff in Cottingham, Stoothoff, and Murdoch 1985: I, 111–151.

1641.   *Meditations on First Philosophy*, trans. by John Cottingham in Cottingham, Stoothoff, and Murdoch 1985: II, 3–62.

1644. *Principles of Philosophy*, in Cottingham, Stoothoff, and Murdoch 1985: I, 179–291.

1649. *Les Passions de l'Ame* (1ˢᵗ ed.; Paris: Henry Le Gras); trans. by Stephen H. Voss as *The Passions of the Soul* (Indianapolis, IN: Hackett Publishing Co., 1988).

DOYLE, John P., Editor and Translator.

2001. *The Conimbricenses: Some Questions on Signs* (Milwaukee, WI: Marquette University Press). Critical edition in bilingual format of Conimbricenses 1607, q.v.

ECO, Umberto.

1976. *A Theory of Semiotics*, trans. David Osmond-Smith (Bloomington: Indiana University Press).

EMMECHE, Claus.

1994. *The Garden in the Machine* (Princeton, NJ: Princeton University Press).

ENGLER, Rudolf.

1962. "Théorie et critique d'un principe saussurien: l'arbitraire du signe", *Cahiers Ferdinard de Saussure* 19, 5–66.

FISCH, Max H. (21 December 1900–1995 January 6).

1986. "Philodemus and Semeiosis (1879–1883)", section 5 (pp. 329–330) of the essay "Peirce's General Theory of Signs", in *Peirce, Semeiotic, and Pragmatism. Essays by Max H. Fisch*, ed. Kenneth Laine Ketner and Christian J. W. Kloesel (Bloomington, IN: Indiana University Press, 1986), 321–356.

FITZGERALD, Desmond J. (1924–)

1986. "The Semiotic of John Poinsot", paper on the *Tractatus* in *Semiotics 1986* (Proceedings of the 11th Annual Meeting of the Semiotic Society of America), ed. John Deely and Jonathan Evans (Lanham, MD: University Press of America, 1987), 430–433.

1986a. "John Poinsot's *Tractatus de Signis*", *Journal of the History of Philosophy* XXVI.1 (January), 146–149.

FRISCH, Karl von.

1967. *The Dance Language and Orientation of Bees* (Cambridge, MA).

GALILEO GALILEI (15 February 1564–1642 January 8).
> 1632. *Dialogue concerning the Two Chief World Systems*, trans. Stillman Drake, with a Foreword by Albert Einstein (2nd ed.; Berkeley: University of California Press, 1967).

GROTE, George (17 November 1794–1871 June 18).
> 1872. *Aristotle*, posthumous ed. by Alexander Bain and G. Croom Robinson (London: J. Murray), 2 vols.

GUAGLIARDO, Vincent (14 September 1944–1995 August 13).
> 1993. "Being and Anthroposemiotics", in *Semiotics 1993*, ed. Robert Corrington and John Deely (Lanham, MD: University Press of America, 1994), 50–56.

HAUSDORFF, Felix (8 November 1868–1942 January 26): *see* MONGRÉ, Paul (the *nom de plume* under which Hausdorff introduced the expression "semiotisches Thier").

HEIDEGGER, Martin (26 September 1889–1976 May 26).
> 1927. *Sein und Zeit*, Erste Hälfte, originally published in the *Jahrbuch für Phänomenologie und phänomenologische Forschung*, ed. E. Husserl (Halle), VIII, 1–438; English trans. from the 7th German ed. (Tübingen: Neomarius Verlag) by John Macquarrie and Edward Robinson as *Being and Time* (New York: Harper & Row, 1962). Page references in the present work are to pagination of the 8th German ed., as given in the margins and cross-references of the Macquarrie & Robinson English trans.
> 1943. *Vom Wesen der Wahrheit* (Frankfurt: Klostermann, 1954; actual composition 1930). The English translation by R. F. C. Hull and Alan Crick, "On the Essence of Truth", in *Existence and Being*, ed. Werner Brock (Chicago: Gateway, 1949), pp. 292–324, was particularly consulted in preparing the present work.
> 1947. *Platons Lehre von der Wahrheit, mit einem Brief über den Humanismus* (Bern: Francke).

HOFFMEYER, Jesper.
> 1993. "Biosemiotics and ethics", in Witoszek and Gulbrandsen eds. 1993: 152–175; reprinted in *Biopolitics. A Feminist and Ecological Reader on Biotechnology*, ed. Vandana Shiva and Ingunn Moser (London, UK: Zed Books, 1995), 141–161.
> 1996. *Signs of Meaning in the Universe* (Bloomington, IN: Indiana University Press), trans. by Barbara J. Haverland of *En Snegl*

På Vejen: Betydningens naturhistorie (Copenhagen: Rosinante, 1993).

2000. "The Central Dogma: A Joke that Became Real", the 3rd Sebeok Fellow address, delivered 29 September 2000 at the SSA Annual Meeting held at Purdue University; published in *Semiotica* 138–1/4 (2002): 1–13.

2008. *Biosemiotics. An Examination into the Signs of Life and the Life of Signs* (= Approaches to Postmodernity, vol. 2; Scranton, PA: University of Scranton Press), trans. from the Danish *Biosemiotik. En afhandling om livets tegn og tegnenes liv* (Charlottenlund, Denmark: Forlaget Ries, 2005) by Jesper Hoffmeyer and Donald Favareau, ed. Donald Favareau.

HOFFMEYER, Jesper, and Claus EMMECHE, Guest-Editors.
1999. *Biosemiotics*, Special Issue of *Semiotica* 127.

JAKI, Stanley (17 August 1924–2009 April 7).
1999. *Means to Message: A Treatise on Truth* (Grand Rapids, MI: Eerdmans).

KESSEL, Edward L. (1945–1959)
1955. "The Mating Activities of Balloon Flies", *Systematic Zoology* 4 (1955), 96–104.

KRAMPEN, Martin (1928–).
1981. "Phytosemiotics", *Semiotica*, 36.3/4: 187-209. Substantially reprinted in Deely, Williams, and Kruse 1986: 83–95.

KULL, Kalevi, Guest-Editor.
2001. *Jakob von Uexküll: A Paradigm for Biology and Semiotics*, a Special Issue of *Semiotica* 134–1/4.

LÉVINAS, Emmanuel (12 January 1906–1995 December 25).
1967. *En découvrant l'existence avec Husserl et Heidegger* (expanded 2nd ed.; Paris: Vrin).

LOCKE, John (29 April 1632–1704 October 28).
1690. *An Essay Concerning Humane Understanding* (London: Printed by Elizabeth Holt for Thomas Basset). The concluding chapter introducing the term "semiotic" into the English language has been photographically reproduced from the copy of the original edition located at the Lilly Library of Indiana University, Bloomington, at least three times recently, in: Deely, Williams, and Kruse 1986: 2–4; Deely 1993; Deely

1994a: 112. It has also been published in parallel column with the Burridge Latin translation of 1701 in Deely 2004.

MARKOŠ, Anton, Filip GRYGAR, László HAJNAL, Karel KLEISNER, Zdeněk KRATOCHIVÍL, and Zdeněk NEUBAUER.

2009. *Life as Its Own Designer. Darwin's origin and Western thought* (Dordrecht, Netherlands: Springer).

MARITAIN, Jacques (18 November 1882–1973 April 28).

1937–1938. "Sign and Symbol", trans. Mary Morris for the *Journal of the Warburg Institute* I, 1–11.

1938. "Signe et Symbole", *Revue Thomiste* XLIV (April), 299–330.

1943. "Sign and Symbol", English trans. by H. L. Binsse of 1938 entry above q.v., but with footnotes separated from the text proper at the end of the volume, in *Redeeming the Time* (London: Geoffrey Bles), text pp. 191–224, Latin notes pp. 268–276.

1947. *The Person and the Common Good*, trans. John J. Fitzgerald (New York: Charles Scribner's Sons).

1953. Letter to Yves Simon, dated 28 April, and published as the "Preface" to *The Material Logic of John of St. Thomas. Basic Treatises*, trans. by Yves R. Simon, John J. Glanville, and G. Donald Hollenhorst (Chicago: University of Chicago Press, 1955), pp. v–viii. (Unhappily, Simon and his colleagues translate the exclusive and exhaustive alternative between *relatio secundum esse and dici* at the basis of Poinsot's doctrine of signs as though it presented three rather than two alternatives, a disaster which I have noted in the 1985 independent edition from Poinsot 1632 [117 note 6] to prevent readers who have access only to the Simon English [1955: 389, second full paragraph on page] from being led astray by this false rendering — a rendering which makes Poinsot's semiotic actually impossible to grasp for anyone relying on that English text alone, which provides a tragic if paradigm instance of "*traduttore, traditore*".)

1956. "Le Langage et la Theorie du Signe", Annexe au Chapitre II of *Quatre Essais sur l'Esprit dans sa Condition Charnelle* (nouvelle edition revue et augmentee; Paris: Alsatia), 113–124. This chapter II is the text of the entry for 1938 above, but without the annex.

1957. "Language and the Theory of Sign", in *Language: An Enquiry into Its Meaning and Function*, ed. Ruth Nanda Anshen (New York: Harper and Brothers), 86–101, referred to in the enhanced 1986 reprint, as explained in the following two paragraphs.

Anshen's 1957 Maritain essay is an English version of the French text of the Maritain 1956 entry preceding, but with several paragraphs added (apparently by Maritain himself) near the beginning to make the essay self-contained when published apart from the French 1938 main essay text which accompanied the 1956 French text. The added opening paragraphs are a summary of the opening section entitled "The Theory of the Sign" (in 1943: 191–195). That 1943 English text (French 1938) had appended extensive Latin endontes drawn from Poinsot's 1632 treatise on signs, nothing of which appears in the Anshen English.

The 1957 Anshen English text, then, but with the full Poinsot 1632 references restored (in footnote rather than endnote form), and with some glosses added from the 1943 English trans. of Maritain 1938, is presented as an enhanced reprint — "enhanced" here meaning, thus, the addition of a full technical apparatus explicitly connecting the essay to Maritain's work on semiotic begun in 1937 and to the text of Poinsot 1632 on which Maritain centrally drew — in Deely, Kruse, and Williams, eds., 1986: 51–62. References in the present book are based on this 1986 enhanced reprint.

MATSON, Wallace I. (1921–)
1987. *A New History of Philosophy* (New York: Harcourt Brace Jovanovich), in two volumes.

MANETTI, Giovanni (1 June 1949–).
1987. *Le teorie del segno nell'antichità classica* (Milan: Bompiani), trans. by Christine Richardson as *Theories of the Sign in Classical Antiquity* (Bloomington, IN: Indiana University Press, 1993).

MARTINELLI, Dario.
2002. *How Musical Is a Whale? Towards a Theory of Zoömusicology* (Acta Semiotica Fennica XIII; Imatra, Finland: International Semiotics Institute).

MESSNER, Johannes (16 February 1891–1984 February 12).
>   1965.   *Social Ethics: Natural Law in the Western World,* trans. by J. J.
>   Doherty (rev. ed.; St. Louis: Herder).

MONGRÉ, Paul (= Felix Hausdorff, German mathematician, 1868–
1942)
>   1897.   *Sant' Ilario. Gedanken aus der Lanschaft Zarathustras* (Leipzig:
>   C. G. Naumann), p. 7, ¶7.
>
>   This early usage by Hausdorff fits well with the thesis that
>   postmodernity in philosophy (for which the definition of
>   human being as semiotic animal replaces the modern defini-
>   tion as *res cogitans*) should be dated from May 14 of 1867: see
>   Deely 2001: 637.

NÖTH, Winfried, Organizer.
>   2001.   German-Italian Colloquium "The Semiotic Threshold from
>   Nature to Culture", Kassell, Germany, 16–17 February at
>   the Center for Cultural Studies, University of Kassel; papers
>   published together with the Imatra 2000 Ecosemiotics col-
>   loquium in *The Semiotics of Nature,* a Special Issue of *Sign
>   System Studies* 29.1, ed. Kalevi Kull and Winfried Nöth. (This
>   journal, founded by Juri Lotman in 1967, is the oldest con-
>   temporary journal of semiotics, and, interestingly, appeared
>   in its first three issues under the original version of Locke's
>   coinage, Σημίωτική).
>   2001a.   "Ecosemiotics and the Semiotics of Nature", *Sign System
>   Studies* 29.1, 71–82.

PEIRCE, Charles Sanders (10 September 1839–1914 April 19).
>   1867.   "On a New List of Categories", *Proceedings of the Ameri-
>   can Academy of Arts and Sciences* 7 (presented 14 May 1867),
>   287–298; in CP 1.545–559, with "notes on the preceding"
>   continuing to 1.567 (Burks p. 261); and in W 2.49–59.
>
>   Gloss from a 4 April 2009 email of André De Tienne:
>   "The year of publication of the 'New List of Categories'
>   (NLC) is technically 1868, the year of publication of volume
>   7 of the AAAS Proceedings (which contained 5 papers by
>   Peirce on logic, all presented to AAAS meetings through-
>   out 1867). They were printed (as opposed to 'published') in
>   1867, however, and Peirce had offprints made for himself
>   toward the end of 1867. In particular, he had the first three

papers (the third being NLC) bound together under the title 'Three papers on Logic', and he was distributing copies of that set to friends in November 1867."

1903. Lowell Lectures, "Some Topics of Logic Bearing on Questions Now Vexed", esp.: lect. IIIA, "Lessons from the History of Philosophy", CP 1.15–26; draft 3 of lect. 3 entitled "Degenerate Cases", in CP 1.521–544; lect. 8, "How To Theorize", CP 5.590–604 (Burks p. 295); and the section published in CP 4.510–529 under the title "The Gamma Part of Existential Graphs".

1904. "On Signs and the Categories", from a letter to Lady Welby dated 12 October, in CP 8.327–341 (Burks p. 321).

1905/1906. Ms. 283, partially published under the title "The Basis of Pragmaticism" in CP 1.573-574 (= ms. pp. 37–45), 5.549–554 (=ms. pp. 45-59), and 5.448n. (=ms. pp. 135-148) (Burks p. 328 and 298).

PETRILLI, Susan.

1998. *Teoria dei Segni e del Linguaggio* (Bari, Italy: Edizioni B. A. Graphis).

2003. "Responsibility of Power and the Power of Responsibility: From the 'Semiotic' to the 'Semioethic' Animal", presented in the Friday, 26 September section "Ethik & Orientierung" / "Ethics & Orientation" of the "Macht der Zeichen, Zeichen der Macht / Signs of Power, Power of Signs" international interdisciplinary symposium held as a Festschrift in honor of Jeff Bernard under joint ISSS and IASS-AIS sponsorship in Vienna 26–28 September 2003; in Withalm and Wallmannsberger, eds. 2004: 103–119.

2007. *Semiotics Today: From Global Semiotics to Semioethics, a Dialogic Response* (Ottawa, Canada: Legas).

2009. "Understanding global communication in today's world: global semiotics and semioethics", in *Communication: Understanding/Misunderstanding*, ed. Eero Tarasti in association with Paul Forsell and Richard Littlefield (Acta Semiotica Fennica XXXIV, Proceedings of the 9th Congress of the IASS/AIS–Helsinki-Imatra, 11–17 June 2007; Imatra: International Semiotics Institute, 2009), 1365–1371.

2009a. "Semiotics as semioethics in the era of global communication", *Semiotica* 173.1–4, 343–367.

PETRILLI, Susan, and Augusto PONZIO.

    2001.   *Thomas Sebeok and the Signs of Life* (Great Britain: Icon Books).

    2003.   *Semioetica* (Rome: Meltemi).

    2004.   "Semioethics and the symptomatology of globalization. Global communication in the perspective of global semiotics", presented Sunday, July 11, as part of Round Table 008 "Issues in Socio-Semiotics" of the 8th IASS Congress, Lyon, France, 7–12 July 2004, at Université Lumière Lyon 2, sponsored by the International Rossi-Landi Network (FRIN).

    2009.   "Semioethics", *The Routledge Companion to Semiotics*, ed. Paul Cobley (London: Routledge), 150–162.

PHILODEMUS (C.110–C.40BC).

    i.54–40BC.   Περὶ σημειώσεων (*De Signis*), trans. as *On the Methods of Inference* in the ed. of Phillip Howard De Lacy and Estelle Allen De Lacy, rev. with the collaboration of Marcello Gigante, Francesco Longo Auricchio, and Adele Tepedino Guerra (Naples: Bibliopolis, 1978), Greek text pp. 27–87, English 91–131.

PIEPER, Josef (4 May 1904–1997 November 6).

    1952.   *Leisure: The Basis of Culture*, new English trans. by Gerald Malsbary (orig. ed. 1952; South Bend, IN: St Augustine's Press, 1998).

PITTS, Walter, and Warren S. McCULLOCH.

    1947.   "How We Know Universals: The Perception of Auditory and Visual Forms", *Bulletin of Mathematical Biophysics* 9, 127–149.

POINSOT, John (9 June 1589–1644 June 17).

    Note. A complete table of all the editions, complete and partial, and in whatever language, of Poinsot's systematic works in philosophy and theology is provided in Deely 1985: 396–397. A complete breakdown of the contents of the original volumes of Poinsot's *Cursus Theologicus* and of the relation of that content to the volumes of the principal modern editions is provided in Deely 1994: 284. The principal modern edition referred to in this work is abbreviated as R followed by a volume number (I, II, or III) and pages, with column (a or b) and line indications as needed = the *Cursus Philosophicus*

Thomisticus, ed. by B. Reiser in 3 volumes (Turin: Marietti, 1930, 1933, 1937).

1631. *Artis Logicae Prima Pars* (Alcalá, Spain). The opening pages 1–11a14 of this work and the "Quaestio Disputanda I. De Termino. Art. 6. Utrum Voces Significant per prius Conceptus an Res" pages 104b31–108a33, relevant to the discussion of signs in the *Secunda Pars* of 1632 (entry following), have been incorporated in the 1632a entry (second entry following, q.v., pp. 4–30 and 342–351 "Appendix A. On the Signification of Language", respectively), for the independent edition of that discussion published by the University of California Press. From R I: 1–247.

1632. *Artis Logicae Secunda Pars* (Alcalá, Spain). From R I: 249–839.

1632a. *Tractatus de Signis*, subtitled *The Semiotic of John Poinsot*, extracted from the *Artis Logicae Prima et Secunda Pars* of 1631–1632 (above two entries) using the text of the emended second impression (1932) of the 1930 Reiser edition (Turin: Marietti), and arranged in bilingual format by John Deely in consultation with Ralph A. Powell (First Edition; Berkeley: University of California Press, 1985), as explained in Deely 1985, q.v. Pages in this volume are set up in matching columns of English and Latin, with intercolumnar numbers every fifth line. (Thus, references are by page number, followed by a slash and appropriate line number of the specific section of text referred to — e.g., 287/3–26.)

Pages in this volume are set up in matching columns of English and Latin, with intercolumnar numbers every fifth line. (Thus, references are by page number, followed by a slash and appropriate line number of the specific section of text referred to — e.g., 287/3–26.) The work is also available as a full-text database, stand-alone on floppy disk or combined with an Aquinas database, as an Intelex Electronic Edition (Charlottesville, VA: Intelex Corp., 1992).

PONZIO, Augusto.

2009. *Emmanuel Levinas, Globalisation, and Preventive Peace* (Ottawa, Canada: Legas).

PORPHYRY THE PHOENICIAN (c.232–301/6).
c.AD271.*Porphyrii Isagoge et in Aristotelis Categorias Commentarium* (Greek text), ed. A. Busse (Berlin, 1887); English trans. by Edward W. Warren, *Porphyry the Phoenician: Isagoge* (Toronto: Pontifical Institute of Mediaeval Studies, 1975).

RATZINGER, Joseph (16 March 1927– ; Pope Benedict XVI as of 19 April 2005).
1970.	*Introduction to Christianity* (New York: Herder and Herder).
2009.	June 29 encyclical letter "Caritas in Veritate" (Pope Benedict XVI; Vatican City).

RAUCH, Irmengard, and Gerald F. CARR, Eds.
1980.	*The Signifying Animal* (Bloomington: Indiana University Press).

ROSSI-LANDI, Ferruccio (1 March 1921–1985 May 5).
1978.	*Ideologia* (Milan: ISEDI; reprinted Milan: Mondadori, 1982; and with a new Introduction by Augusto Ponzio, Rome: Meltemi, 2005). Trans. into English by R. Griffin as *Marxism and Ideology* (Oxford: Clarendon Press, 2005)

SANTAELLA (= SANTAELLA-BRAGA), Lúcia.
1994.	"The Way to Postmodernity", Preface to Deely 1994: xi–xiii.

SAUSSURE, Ferdinand de.
1916.	*Cours de Linguistique Générale*, publié par Charles Bally et Albert Sechehaye avec la collaboration de Albert Reidlinger (Paris: Librarie Payot & Cⁱᵉ).

SCHMITZ, Kenneth L. (1922–).
1990.	"Postmodern or modern-plus?", *Communio* 17 (Summer), 152–166.

SCHRADER, George.
1967.	"The Thing in Itself in Kantian Philosophy", in *Kant. A Collection of Critical Essays*, ed. Robert Paul Wolff (Notre Dame, IN: University of Notre Dame Press).

SEBEOK, Thomas A. (9 November 1920–2001 December 21).
1971.	"'Semiotic' and Its Congeners", in *Linguistic and Literary Studies in Honor of Archibald Hill, I: General and Theoretical Linguistics*, ed. Mohammed Ali Jazayery, Edgar C. Polomé, and Werner Winter (Lisse, Netherlands: Peter de Ridder

Press), 283–295; reprinted in Deely, Williams and Kruse 1986: 255–263.

1975. "The Semiotic Web: A Chronicle of Prejudices", *Bulletin of Literary Semiotics* 2 (December), 1–65; "Index of Names" added *ibid.* 3 (May, 1976), 25–28.

1975a. "Zoosemiotics: At the Intersection of Nature and Culture", in *The Tell-Tale Sign*, ed. T. A. Sebeok (Lisse, the Netherlands: Peter de Ridder Press), pp. 85–95; reprinted in Sebeok 1976, 1985.

1975b. "Six Species of Signs: Some Propositions and Strictures", *Semiotica* 13.3, 233–260; reprinted in Sebeok 1976, 1985: 117–142, which reprint is referred to throughout the present book.

1976. *Contributions to the Doctrine of Signs* (Bloomington, IN, and Lisse, Netherlands: Publication of the Research Center for Language and Semiotic Studies of Indiana University, together with The Peter De Ridder Press). Reprinted with an extended Prefatory Essay by Brooke Williams, "Challenging Signs at the Crossroads", evaluating the book in light of major reviews (=Sources in Semiotics IV; Lanham, MD: University Press of America, 1985).

1979. "Prefigurements of Art", *Semiotica* 27–1/3, 3–73.

1984. "Vital Signs", Presidential Address delivered October 12 to the ninth Annual Meeting of the Semiotic Society of America, Bloomington, Indiana, October 11–14; subsequently printed in *The American Journal of Semiotics* 3.3, 1–27, and reprinted in Sebeok 1986: 59–79, to which page references in the present essay are keyed.

1984a. June 3. "The Evolution of Communication and the Origin of Language", lecture in the June 1–3 ISISSS '84 Colloquium on "Phylogeny and Ontogeny of Communication Systems". Published under the title "Communication, Language, and Speech. Evolutionary Considerations", in Sebeok 1986: 10–16.

1984b. "Symptom", Chapter 10 of *New Directions in Linguistics and Semiotics*, ed. James E. Copeland (Houston: Rice University Studies), 212–230.

1985. *Contributions to the Doctrine of Signs* (=Sources in Semiotics IV; reprint of 1976 original with an extended Preface by Brooke Williams, "Challenging Signs at the Crossroads", evaluating the book in light of major reviews; Lanham, MD: University Press of America).

1985a.   "Vital Signs", *American Journal of Semiotics*, 3.3 (1985), 1–27.

1986.   *I Think I Am A Verb: More Contributions to the Doctrine of Signs* (New York: Plenum Press).

1989.   *The Sign & Its Masters* (2ⁿᵈ ed.; Lanham, MD: University Press of America).

1989a.   "Ernst Cassirer, Jacques Maritain, and Susanne Langer", in *Semiotics 1989,* ed. John Deely, Karen Haworth, Terry Prewitt (Lanham, MD: University Press of America, 1990), 389–397.

1989b.   "Semiotics in the United States", in *The Semiotic Web 1989*, co-edited with Jean Umiker-Sebeok (Berlin: Mouton de Gruyter, 1990), 275–398.

1991.   *Semiotics in the United States* (Bloomington, IN: Indiana University Press).

1996.   "An Interview with Professor Sebeok on Semiotics (October, 1996)", conducted and transcribed by Laura Shintani, in *Sign: aliquid stat pro aliquo* (Toronto Student Journal of Semiotic Studies, First Edition, ISSN 1138–160X; University of Toronto: Program in Semiotics and Communication Theory, 2000), 48–57. The transcription is rough and incomplete, but a valuable statement over-all.

2001.   *Global Semiotics* (Bloomington, IN: Indiana University Press).

2001a.   "Biosemiotics: Its Roots, Proliferation, and Prospects", in Kull Guest-Ed. 2001: 61–78.

SOKOLOWSKI, Robert.

2002.   "Semiotics in Husserl's Logical Investigations", in *One Hundred Years of Phenomenology*, ed. Dan Zahavi and Frederik Stjernfelt. (Dordrecht and Boston: Kluwer Academic Publishers), 171–183.

TARASTI, Eero.

2000.   *Existential Semiotics* (Bloomington, IN: Indiana University Press).

TØNNESSEN, Morten.

2003.   "Umwelt Ethics", *Sign System Studies* 31.1, 281–299.

TODOROV, Tzvetan (1939–).
    1977.   "The Birth of Occidental Semiotics", being "La naissance de la sémiotique occidentale", pp. 13–58 of Todorov's *Théories du symbole* (Paris: Éditions du Seuil, 1977), trans. by Daphne Swabey and Judith Mullen, in *The Sign*, ed. Richard W. Bailey, L. Matejka, and P. Steiner (Ann Arbor, MI: Michigan Slavic Publications, 1978), 1–42.

TRABANT, Jürgen (25 October 1942–).
    2004.   *Vico's New Science of Ancient Signs: A Study of Sematology*, trans. from German by Sean Ward (London: Routledge).

VETLESEN, Arne Johan.
    1994.   *Perception, Empathy, and Judgment. An inquiry into the preconditions of moral performance* (University Park, PA: Pennsylvania State University Press).

VON FRISCH, Karl (20 November 1886–1982 June 12).
    1967.   *The Dance Language and Orientation of Bees* (Cambridge, MA).

VON UEXKÜLL, Thure (15 March 1908–2004 September 29).
    1982.   "Semiotics and the Problem of the Observer", in *Semiotics 1982*, ed. John Deely and Jonathan Evans (Lanham, MD: University Press of America, 1987), 3–12.

WETLESEN, Jon.
    1993.   "Who Has a Moral Status in the Environment?", in Witoszek and Gulbrandsen eds. 1993: 98–129.

WILLIAMS DEELY, Brooke.
    1982.   "The Historian as Observer", in *Semiotics 1982*, ed. John Deely and Jonathan Evans (Lanham, MD: University Press of America, 1987), 13–25.
    2008.   "Teresa of Avila: Time for a Semiosis beyond Feminism", *Semiotics 2008* (Proceedings of the 33rd Annual Meeting of the Semiotic Society of America; Ottawa, Canada: Legas, 2009), 34–47.
    2010.   "Thomas A. Sebeok: On Semiotics of History and History of Semiotics", in Paul Cobley, John Deely, Kalevi Kull, and Susan Petrilli, eds., *Semiotics Continues to Astonish ... How Thomas A. Sebeok shaped the future of the doctrine of signs*, ed.

Paul Cobley, John Deely, Kalevi Kull, and Susan Petrilli (Berlin: Mouton de Gruyter).

WITHALM, Gloria, and Josef WALLMANNSBERGER, eds.

2004.   *Macht der Zeichen, Zeichen der Macht/Signs of Power, Power of Signs* (Festschrift für Jeff Bernard; =Trans-Studien zur Veraenderung der Welt 3; Wien: Lit.Verlag).

WITOSZEK, Nina, and Elizabeth GULBRANDSEN, Editors.

1993.   *Culture and Environment: Interdisciplinary Approaches*, (Nature and Humanities Series 1; Oslo, Norway: Centre for Development and the Environment, Centre for Technology and Culture, University of Oslo).

WOJTYŁA, Karol Jósef (= Pope John-Paul II; 18 May 1920–2005 April 2).

1978.   "Subjectivity and the Irreducible in Man", in *Analecta Husserliana* 7 (1978), 104–114.

1998.   *Fides et Ratio*, encyclical letter on the relationship between faith and reason (Rome, Italy: Vatican City, September 14).

Index

COLOPHON

Typesetting by Marty Klaif

Graphic design consultation with Czeslaw Jan Grycz

Composed in Adobe InDesign CS4
using Bembo for body text, and Graeca II for Greek text

On a 36 × 54 pica trim size, the image area is 24 × 43.5 picas
with margins of 5p3 inside, 3p top, 6p9 outside, 7p6 bottom;
top/bottom margins become 6p/4p9 on pages with drop folios

Chaper titles are 16/22,
subheads are italic 12/14.4 with 1p above and 0p6 below;
body text is 11/14; extracts are 10.5/13 with 0p8 above and below;
running headers and footers are 10;
footnotes are 9/10.8 with 0p3 separation;
references are 10/12.5; the index is 8/8.8

Drops on the chapter title pages are
12p to the chapter title, and 22p6 to the text;
drop to the text on other pages is 5p6